D1245381

REENGINEERING THE DISTRIBUTOR

Eugene R. Roman

Roman, Eugene R.
    Reengineering the Distributor

ISBN 0-9649974-0-1

DEDICATION

*In memory of my dear friend
and business associate
Leonard Urlik,
whose valuable input not only contributed
to this publication,
but enhanced my overall knowledge
of the distribution industry*

*and to
my wife, Sandie,
without whose help and support
this book would never have been published.*

- Gene Roman

CONTENTS

FOREWORD

Buy this book. It offers pragmatic, how-to solutions for applying every state-of-the-art electronic application to a distributor's business. The book has no fluff or global generalities, just straightforward opportunities and solutions. The level of detail goes down to pictures of the computer screen that Gene Roman's client distributors actually use.

Because Gene covers many applications, there will be one or more topics that will speak directly to each functional manager at a distribution center. But, they should at least skim through the rest of the applications because they all add up to first understanding cross-departmental processes and then the why and how of reengineering them. It would also be an excellent educational read or syllabus for any distribution management trainee.

With this book, Gene has made a unique contribution to the distribution industry at a time of need. The book is the fruition of his 20+ years working with distributors to offer them the best, latest and most practical information-technology solutions. Those distributors who are looking for solutions to help them deal with hyper-competition will be very pleased with their investment in this book.

D. Bruce Merrifield, Jr.

WHY I WROTE THIS BOOK

I wrote this book because it will show you how to reengineer your business. Many books tell you what reengineering is, but not how to do it. This is like going to a convention and hearing an expert talk, or hearing a motivational speaker. You get all pumped up for about 90 minutes, you take some notes, and you remember 1% to 3% of what was said. If the speaker was humorous and/or entertaining, as you are leaving the room, you and the person next to you discuss how good the session was. By the end of the next session, you forgot what was said and what you were going to do! How much will you be able to implement?

Hammer and Champy wrote a fabulous book titled *Reengineering the Corporation,* which inspired me to write this book. They wrote about large corporations such as Taco Bell, Kodak, Ford, Hewlett Packard, Otis Elevator, Proctor & Gamble, Hallmark, and AEtna Life & Casualty. You may not have a lot in common with these companies, but as a distributor, you do need to reengineer. *Reengineering the Distributor* is intended to help you streamline the basic processes that are necessary to run your business. You must forget the old way of doing business and have an open mind to new ideas.

I had a professor in graduate school who used a ruler to grade papers: the thicker, the better. I have read business books just like that. The author feels he has to give you your money's worth in volume, not content. I wrote this book as concisely and to the point as possible. Your time is valuable.

WHAT IS REENGINEERING ALL ABOUT?

Reengineering is not just about changing the way you do things. It is not about incremental improvements. It is not fixing procedures, functions, and tasks. It is not about improving the efficiency of a single department. Would you be happy with an increase in revenue per employee from $225,000 to $300,000? If so, you do not need to reengineer.

Reengineering means beginning with a clean slate; taking a blank piece of paper and starting over. It means looking at processes, not functions, or departments, or jobs, or tasks.

Why do you do what you do the way you do it?

The first step is to ask your employees, your department managers, or yourself, "Why do we do that...that way?" The answer is probably:

A. Because that's the way we've always done it.
B. I don't know.
C. I don't remember.

If so, then it's time to reengineer.

Reengineering is not a new concept. I have been working for and consulting with distributors and manufacturers for over 25 years, but only after reading _Reengineering the Corporation_ did I realize that I have been reengineering distributors' processes for quite some time. You could call it getting back to basics (or simplifying processes).

Hammer and Champy gave an illustration in their book about how Ford Motor Company, through reengineering, reduced their Accounts Payable Department from 500 people to 125 people.

In the early 1980s, Ford, like many other American corporations, was searching for ways to cut overhead and administrative costs. One of the places Ford believed it could reduce costs was in its accounts payable department, the organization that paid the bills submitted by Ford's suppliers. At that time, Ford's North American accounts payable department employed more than five hundred people. By using computers to automate some functions, Ford executives believed that they could attain a 20 percent head-count reduction in the department, bringing the number of clerks down to four hundred. By our definition, this incremental improvement, achieved by automating the existing manual process, would not qualify as business reengineering. Nonetheless, Ford managers thought 20 percent sounded good -- until they visited Mazda.

Ford had recently acquired a 25 percent equity interest in the Japanese company. The Ford executives noted that the admittedly smaller company took care of its accounts payable chores with only five people. The contrast - Ford's five hundred people to Mazda's five - was too great to attribute just to the smaller company's size, esprit de corps, company songs, or morning calisthenics. Automating to achieve a 20 percent personnel reduction clearly would not put Ford on a cost-par with

Mazda, so the Ford executives were forced to rethink the entire process in which the accounts payable department took part.

This decision marked a critical shift in perspective for Ford, because companies can reengineer only business processes, not the administrative organizations that have evolved to accomplish them. "Accounts payable" cannot be reengineered, because it is not a process. It is a department, an organizational artifact of a particular process design. The accounts payable department consists of a group of clerks sitting in a room and passing paper amongst themselves. They cannot be reengineered, but what they do can be - and the way they are eventually reorganized to accomplish the new work process will follow from the requirements of the reengineered process itself.

We cannot emphasize this crucial distinction enough. Reengineering must focus on redesigning a fundamental business process, not on departments or other organizational units. Define a reengineering effort in terms of an organization unit, and the effort is doomed. Once a real work process is reengineered, the shape of the organizational structure required to perform the work will become apparent. It probably will not look much like the old organization; some departments or other organizational units may even disappear, as they did at Ford.

The process that Ford eventually reengineered was not "accounts payable," but "procurement." That process took as input a purchase order from, say, a plant that needed parts and provided that plant (the process customer) with bought-and-paid-for goods. The procurement process included the accounts payable function, but it also encompassed purchasing and receiving.

Ford's old parts acquisition process was remarkably conventional. It began with the purchasing department sending a purchase order to a vendor, with a copy going to accounts payable. When the vendor shipped the goods and they arrived at Ford, a clerk at the receiving dock would complete a form describing the goods and send it to accounts payable. The vendor, meanwhile, sent accounts payable an invoice.

Accounts payable now had three documents relating to these goods - the purchase order, the receiving document, and the invoice. If all three matched, a clerk issued payment. Most of the time, that is what happened, but occasionally Vilfredo Pareto intervened.

Pareto, an early twentieth-century Italian economist, formulated what most of us call the 80-20 rule, technically known as the law of mal-distribution. This rule states that 80 percent of the effort expended in a process is caused by only 20 percent of the input. In the case of Ford's accounts payable department, clerks there spent the great majority of their time straightening out the infrequent situations in which the documents - purchase order, receiving document, and invoice - did not match. Sometimes, the resolution required weeks of time and enormous amounts of work in order to trace and clarify the discrepancies.

Ford's new accounts payable process looks radically different. Accounts payable clerks no longer match purchase order with invoice with receiving document, primarily because the new process eliminates the invoice entirely. The results have proved dramatic. Instead of five hundred people, Ford now has just 125 people involved in vendor payment.

The new process looks like this: When a buyer in the purchasing department issues a purchase order to a vendor, *that buyer simultaneously enters the order into an on-line database. Vendors, as before, send goods to the receiving dock. When they arrive, someone in receiving checks a computer terminal to see whether the received shipment corresponds to an outstanding purchase order in the database. Only two possibilities exist: It does or it doesn't. If it does, the clerk at the dock accepts the goods and pushes a button on the terminal keyboard that tells the database that the goods have arrived. Receipt of the goods is now recorded in the database, and the computer will automatically issue and send a check to the vendor at the appropriate time. If, on the other hand, the goods do not correspond to an outstanding purchase order in the database, the clerk on the dock will refuse the shipment and send it back to the vendor.*

The basic concept of the change at Ford is simple. Payment authorization, which used to be performed by accounts payable, is now accomplished at the receiving dock. The old process fostered Byzantine complexities: searches, suspense files, ticklers - enough to keep five hundred clerks more or less busy. The new process does not. In fact, the new process comes close to eliminating the need for an accounts payable department altogether. In some parts of Ford, such as the Engine Division, the head count in accounts payable is now just 5 percent of its former size. Only a handful of people remains to handle exceptional situations.

The reengineered process at Ford breaks hard and fast rules that formerly applied there. Every business has these rules, deeply ingrained in the operation of the organization, whether they are explicitly spelled out or not.

For instance, Rule One at Ford's accounts payable department was: We pay when we receive the invoice. While this rule was rarely articulated, it was the frame around which the old process was formed. When Ford's managers reinvented this process, they were effectively asking whether they still wanted to live by this rule. The answer was no. The way to break this rule was to eliminate invoices. Instead of "We pay when we receive the invoice," the new rule at Ford is "We pay when we receive the goods." Altering just that one word established the basis for a major business change.[1]

After reading this section, I called one of my clients. Over the past decade I have been assisting them in reengineering elements of their business processes, without realizing it was reengineering. I was simply streamlining processes and eliminating or automating functions using technology.

This client has seven locations, a central warehouse, 30,000 items, 1,000 invoices a day, 15% non-stocks, 250 vendors, and a 98% fill rate. His total purchasing department consists of one buyer and one assistant. The computer automatically creates branch transfers that replenish the branches twice a week, and it also reviews 50 vendors per night, creating purchase orders for all stock and special ordered items as needed. The purchasing function, which is part of the procurement process, had been reengineered, but reengineering the entire process had not been completed.

I asked my client, "How would you like to eliminate the accounts payable function?" I verified that all purchase orders were sent out with prices. I explained the reengineering process Ford did, and he agreed he did not need a vendor invoice to pay the bill. He could pay on receipt.

---

[1]Copyright © 1993 by Michael Hammer and James Champy. Reprinted by permission of HarperCollins Publishers, Inc.

Reengineering is not just about automating current systems. Up until now, most books told you that you had to start with a good manual system, then automate it. That has achieved very little. Technology Consultant Bruce Merrifield states, "Automating existing processes is analogous to paving over cow paths." You can have the fastest invoicing process around, but if you still print four copies of that invoice, you really haven't improved anything.

If you are at all skeptical of what simplifying processes will do to reduce your costs, do the following exercise. Make a list of all of your activities, such as:

1. Deliver orders
2. Cycle Count
3. Provide product information
4. Pull orders
5. Handle customer inquiries
6. Pull transfers
7. Stock material
8. Receive material
9. Process Accounts Payable
10. Issue purchase orders
    Etc.

When you are finished, you should be able to identify 35-40 activities. You will be astounded to discover that approximately 10-14 activities consume about 80% of your costs. If any or all of those activities can be streamlined, eliminated, or automated, your cost savings can be phenomenal. This is a process known as Activity Based Management.

Review the list of all of your activities and then ask yourself for each, "Is this a value-added activity or a non-value-added activity?" Here is a sample:

Activity	Value-Added
Count Stock	N
Research difference	N
Issue PO	Y
Contact Vendor	N
Receive Material	Y
Unload Truck	Y
Inspect	N
Handle Defects	N
Stock Material	Y

Both value-added and non-value-added activities can be very costly; however, you can only be *paid* for value-added activities. The objective of reengineering is to eliminate as many non-value-added activities as possible.

In addition, with the use of technology, some of your more costly value-added activities can be automated. The American Supply Association sponsored an Activity Based Management Project that confirmed that 20% of a distributor's activities account for 80% of his costs. The five most expensive activities of the three distributors studied were identified in a review of the common activities that distributors perform.

Distributor #1 -
1. Deliver Orders
2. Cycle Count
3. Provide Product Information
4. Pick Customer Order
5. Pick and Pack Inside Sales Order

Distributor #2 -
1. Distribute Promotional Materials
2. Pull Transfers
3. Stock Materials
4. Design and Lay Out Ads
5. Handle Customer Inquiries

Distributor #3 -
1. Make Counter Sale
2. Meet with Showroom Customer
3. Process A/P
4. Issue PO
5. Receive Material

Distributor #1's second most costly activity is cycle counting, which is a non-value-added activity. Distributor #3's third most costly activity is process A/P, which is of little value to your customer.

With reengineering, you can find ways to simplify the processes, automate the value-added activities, and eliminate the unnecessary non-value-added activities. We are talking revenues per employee approaching $1,000,000. You cannot accomplish this by shuffling paper. An excellent business process is one that is **simple, mistake proof, and flexible**, and as paperless as possible.

3

THE PROCUREMENT PROCESS

In any distribution business, there are three basic processes: buying, warehousing, and selling. Your real goal is providing your customer (whether he is a retailer, a contractor, or an end user doesn't matter) with goods in a least cost manner. Anything you do to complicate this adds costs. You must reduce his cost of doing business. How many tasks or functions do you do for yourself (that your customer does not care about) that add labor, overhead, and costs?

Your customer does not care if you print six copies of invoices or none. He does not care if you have a complicated commission structure that requires 37 clerks to track. He does not care if you stock a year's supply; he does not care if your shrinkage is 20%, nor does he care if you have six accounts payable clerks, if you have one or ten buyers, if you pay freight or discount your bills. Do you get the picture? The more efficient you are, the lower his cost. He only wants to pay for the value to him.

Let's talk about the procurement process, i.e., sourcing, buying, and paying for it. Keep in mind you and the manufacturer are partners. You are both on the same team and the better your relationship, the better for everyone.

Establishing Vendor Relationships

The most important function of the procurement process is finding the right vendor and then establishing a strategic alliance with that vendor. You will need to be closely tied to your strategic vendors and work together as partners. It is essential that you work together to establish *net* prices that are fair for both parties. Forget all of the complicated rebate programs that add administrative costs.

The Rules

The first thing you need to do is establish the rules by which everyone plays the game. You are the customer. Your vendor cannot be your competition. He is on your team, and if you expect him to be a loyal player, you need to treat him fairly. Do you really need to sell three brands of the same item? All you are doing is adding costs.

Pick The Right Vendor

If your vendor is not technology-driven, then let him know what you expect. If he cannot provide it in an acceptable time frame, then find a vendor who can.

Rule #1 in the Procurement Process

The vendor will bar code the products and use standard UPC compliant numbers, including the each, box, and case labeling indicators.

Two important parts of reengineering in the procurement and warehousing processes are the receiving function and the shipping function. Your goals are *NO PAPER* and *NO ERRORS*. This is impossible to accomplish without bar coding. With today's technology, if your vendor can label his product by printing a part number and description, he can print a bar code. Some vendors have joined the IBCA (Industry Bar Code Alliance) and use UPC (Uniform Product Code) numbers. Others use their manufacturer's code. UPC is preferable, but you should be able to read either. If your vendor cannot or will not provide this basic service, then your costs will increase because you have to receive the old-fashioned way, which is susceptible to errors and increases costs, especially if you have to apply a bar code label yourself. You will need to ask for a price concession of X% (X will vary by company and type of business but 2% is a good start) if your vendor does not bar code.

Rule #2

The vendor must have the capability of doing EDI (Electronic Data Interchange).

EDI will allow you to send your vendor a purchase order without having to mail it, fax it, or talk on the telephone. It will eliminate the need for him to spend money keying your purchase order into his system, and most importantly, it will eliminate any input errors. EDI will allow him to verify electronically that he received your purchase order, and that the prices are correct. His machine will notify your machine of delivery dates without any expediting costs. His machine can also notify your machine when and how many have been shipped. This will allow your automated RF (Radio Frequency) receiving system to detect any discrepancies.

Rule #3

Provide your vendor with information.

You will offer to send sales information to your vendor on a daily, weekly or monthly basis to help him better schedule production, shorten lead time, and reduce back orders. Can you imagine how efficient your vendor could be if he knew (or his computer knew) every day what each of his customers sold and their inventory levels? This is easily accomplished if you are all using the same UPC number and EDI. Sending your vendor sales data on a regular basis can be done using EDI with a transaction set called an "852 Product Activity Data Document." This is a transaction set in VMI (Vendor Managed Inventory).

Rule #4

You do not want a manufacturer's rep (or salesperson) in the channel.

The end user will only pay for goods and services in the distribution channel once, so the days of two or three salespeople getting commission are over. This increases costs. You will never give a salesperson an order verbally or on an order form. In the 1981 DREF (Distribution Research and Education Foundation) Study, it was predicted that the role of the outside sales representative would change. Outside salespersons are becoming more marketing oriented. They need to sell the company and its services, not commodity items. (You may need training and consulting, but you do not need a salesperson.)

Taking the salesperson out of the equation may save you a fair amount of money. You may need a salesperson if the vendor supplies technical or new types of items; however, if the items are commodities, the vendor's salesperson is of little value. The cost can be eliminated, and the savings can be passed on to you and, ultimately, your customers.

I rarely come across a purchasing agent who looks forward to the sales representative coming in to help him "work up an order." Most of the time, the vendor's salesperson just wastes your purchasing agent's time.

Rule #5

You do not want your vendor to waste any money sending you statements or invoices.

Your receiving process will verify (through Radio Frequency scanners in receiving and bar codes on the boxes) that what was received was in fact what was ordered and shipped. Upon receiving, your system will automatically set up the wire transfer to your vendor's account on the appropriate day. You will pay for your purchase through EDI and EFT (Electronic Funds Transfer). (Notice I did not say you would pay his invoice.)

Rule #6

Your vendor must provide you your price changes electronically (not just a list).

Two of the most labor-intensive, and therefore costly, activities you do are keeping prices updated for your stock items and looking through paper catalogs to find special order items. Every vendor has the ability to furnish you *your* prices for each and every item he provides on some electronic media, such as a floppy disk, a CD-ROM, or through the Internet. This means you can create your price levels based on your cost using the power of Excel, and then update your stocking items' prices and costs as well as an on-line electronic catalog with all of your vendor's available parts. By doing this, every one of your employees in customer service or sales can offer a customer his price on a special order part instantly without going to a paper catalog.

Strategic Alliances

Strategic vendor alliances are becoming more and more important in today's distribution pipeline. In order to be a distributor for a vendor, you must form a strategic alliance that is built on trust. Avoiding conflicts and unnecessary procedures is important.

During a meeting with a client, I said, "You must be able to trust your vendor." He replied, "Trust your vendor? Now that's a contradiction in terms!" Do you trust your vendor? If not, then why is he your vendor? Vendors are reducing the number of distributors they want to distribute their product. If you are dealing with one vendor instead of two or three, you must trust him.

Can your vendor trust you? If not, then you do not deserve to be in business, because your customers and employees cannot trust you either.

Strategic alliances are built on trust. If you are going to work toward a common goal, then start with your vendor alliance.

Vendor Performance

In many instances, your vendors' hands are tied when it comes to technology. They are burdened by old batch-oriented mainframes that cannot be changed quickly. (That's like trying to run a race carrying two bowling balls.) Chances are, many of your manufacturers have not reengineered. Many of them are not able to provide you with these cost-saving technology services. If you incur costs because of their inability to service you, ask for concessions.

Remember that you are the customer to the vendor. How important a customer are you? How good a customer are you? If you are an important customer, then you will expect your vendor to earn your business. If he is not performing up to your standards, you need to give him constructive feedback so he can meet your expectations. An example of a vendor performance evaluation is shown on the next page. Discuss your evaluation with your vendor. Pricing errors, shipping errors, and poor service levels are extremely costly.

VENDOR PERFORMANCE REPORT

		Line Items	No. of POs	Serv Level	Orig. Late %	Last Late %	Orig. Avg. Days Late 1	Orig. Avg. Days Late 2	Pricing Errors	Ship. Errors	Returns / Eval.	Total Errors	% of Perfection
Vendor A	Jan	91	11	98.90	6.59	6.59	0.38	0.31	0	0	3	3	96.70
	Feb	118	18	94.92	11.86	8.47	0.31	0.14	1	0	0	1	100.00
	March	106	17	98.11	36.79	36.79	0.59	0.58	1	1	3	5	97.17
	April	131	14	96.97	37.12	37.12	0.27	0.27	0	0	2	0	98.48
	May	143	18	95.80	25.17	24.48	0.37	0.33	3	2	1	6	99.30
Vendor B	Jan	62	45	85.48	59.68	45.16	6.89	3.13	0	0	0	0	100.00
	Feb	59	38	88.14	50.85	42.37	3.12	2.46	0	0	1	0	100.00
	March	64	48	89.06	62.50	51.56	6.84	2.95	1	0	1	2	98.44
	April	60	39	91.67	46.67	41.67	3.95	3.12	2	0	0	2	100.00
	May	61	40	83.61	62.30	40.98	8.08	3.21	0	0	0	1	98.36
Vendor C	Jan	107	26	97.20	76.64	76.64	1.07	0.97	1	4	1	6	99.07
	Feb	88	25	100.00	55.68	54.55	0.53	0.48	2	3	2	7	97.73
	March	122	25	99.18	61.48	51.64	0.72	0.39	7	5	1	13	99.18
	April	104	22	99.04	75.00	74.04	0.62	0.32	3	0	0	3	100.00
	May	123	27	100.00	47.15	36.59	1.72	1.29	2	2	0	4	100.00
Vendor D	Jan	94	20	88.30	39.36	34.04	1.50	1.01	1	2	3	6	96.81
	Feb	86	15	84.88	13.95	10.47	0.79	0.38	2	1	1	4	98.84
	March	109	20	83.49	19.27	17.43	0.87	0.57	1	2	0	3	100.00
	April	188	17	93.09	45.21	39.89	3.01	2.53	0	1	2	3	98.94
	May	102	20	86.27	58.82	42.16	3.91	2.25	0	1	0	1	97.03

If your vendor ships 99.5% accurately and on time, then you will incur very little cost in dealing with that vendor. I've seen distributors who don't even have to check in a vendor's shipment. The vendor is so accurate they simply unload it, put it away, and pay for the shipment.

What's My Price?

Many of you believe that because your vendors have published prices, policies, terms, quantity breaks, and return privileges, they are inflexible. However, strategic vendors, if presented with facts, will work with you.

I was doing consulting for an industrial distributor and worked very closely with his people to make them understand that they had to have a specific GMROI (Gross Margin Return On Investment) for a line to be profitable. I received a call from their branch manager, who was questioning whether or not he should take a one-year contract for 300,000 grinding wheels. His vendor required that he purchase 100,000 at a time. In order to get this contract, his margin on the sale to his customer would be 12%. Because of the 12% margin and the average monthly inventory he would have to carry, his GMROI on this contract would have been .97. As a consultant, I had worked with the management team and stressed that they needed a GMROI of at least 1.3 to be profitable.

Since it was a blanket order, and there was very little chance of the stock becoming obsolete, it still would have been an acceptable deal at .97. However, since he had run a spreadsheet on the data and had the facts and figures, I suggested he call the vendor and tell him that he was going to give away the business to a competitor because of the vendor's requirement to buy 100,000 grinding wheels at a time. His carrying costs would be too high and his GMROI would only be .97, which was unacceptable, based on corporate policy. If the vendor would allow him to buy 50,000 grinding wheels at a time, he would take the business. Of course, the vendor obliged. "Is that all you want?" the vendor said, "I thought you were going to ask for a lower price." When my client re-ran his calculations, his GMROI went from .97 to 1.94 and the transaction became *very profitable* simply by reducing the minimum order quantity he had to buy from 100,000 to 50,000.

Do not expect your vendors to do all the giving. For example, if they can dial in to your system or use EDI to get all the information necessary to reduce your cost and theirs (and serve you better), then you must be ready to accommodate them.

What would your cost be, what would your turns be, how much warehouse space would you need, if your vendor could ship you same day everything you sold today (VMI - Vendor Managed Inventory)? You would only need three to five days worth of inventory. It's here, and it's called Quick Response (QR). Wal-Mart and Lowes are doing it today, and have been since 1989. A satellite dish at each store transmits to the vendor what was sold that day. The manufacturer does not need your purchase order or your buyer; he replenishes what was sold. Why can't your vendor know your ROP (Re-order Point) and what you sell?

Do you have return privileges? Many distributors miss out on vendor return privileges. Depending on how much clout you have with a vendor (which is usually directly proportional to the amount of business you do with him, or how good a negotiator you are), he may let you return 'X' dollars of stock once or twice a year without a restocking fee. Ask him what your return privileges are! Everything is negotiable.

I was consulting with a client who carried a line of tools from a vendor who had a 100 tool minimum purchase, and did not allow him any return privileges. As I returned from lunch one day, the Vice President of Purchasing called me into his office and introduced me to two gentlemen. Since I was finishing another conversation as I walked in, I did not catch their names. He asked me, "Gene, can we live with a GMROI of .75?" I laughed and said, "Joe, you know better than that! What's the line?"

"XYZ Tool," he said.

"Oh," I replied, "they are a terrible vendor. They make you buy 100 tools at a time, and they don't give you any price protection. Your customers can go to the local discount hardware store and buy their product for less than you pay for it. If I were you, I'd call my XYZ salesman and tell him he must do something or you'll change vendors."

Joe turned a bright red, pointed across the desk, and said, "He IS my XYZ salesman!"

Well, I had to recover, so I said to the salesman, "You have the facts. What are you going to do about this?" Then I left as quickly as I could.

About a half-hour later, I saw the XYZ salesman talking with the tool buyer. "Hey," I said jokingly, "don't sell them any more tools. They have too many now."

The salesman came over to tell me he had called the home office to explain the situation. They agreed to allow my client to exchange 100 obsolete items for 100 fast movers. "They have never done that before," the salesman stated, which proved my point. You must track inventory and GMROI and have the ammunition to negotiate better prices, terms, and returns.

Ask yourself what is more costly: to keep those old items on the shelf for a year or two at a 25 to 30 percent annual carrying cost, or to identify these items and pay a 10 percent restocking fee. Obtain a list of excess stock items that have not sold in the last 'X' months and negotiate the best return policy possible.

Purchasing

For those of you who are not ready for QR (Quick Response), you will need to issue purchase orders for a while, so let's discuss purchasing.

Purchasing is a science. If you believe otherwise, you are buying on emotions. If you take the emotion out of buying, then the majority of the purchasing process can be automated.

The computer knows:

1. how many times per month you sell the item
2. the average order size
3. the units sold per month
4. if it's an A, B, C, D, or E item
5. where it's at in its life cycle
6. lead time required to get the item
7. any unusual orders
8. stock-outs (lost sales)
9. how often you can get a stock buy from the vendor
10. the quantity in which you buy (carton, pallet, etc.)
11. the service level
12. how expensive it is

13. your cost of carrying inventory
14. your cost of ordering the item
15. what's on hand, on order, committed, back ordered, and available

How well do you know your inventory?

- Are your stock dollars in A and B (revenue generating) items? Or are they in C, D, and E (unprofitable) items?
- Have you caused this situation by purchasing too many of the wrong items from a vendor to gain some economic advantage?
- Are any of your vendors providing primarily C, D, and E items? If so, should you carry this vendor's line of products?
- Have you had stock-outs on A or B items? Has your present system made you aware of the stock-outs on these items? (Keep in mind that these items account for 70 to 90 percent of your sales!)
- Have you set your ROP (Reorder Point) and EOQ (Economic Order Quantity) to be consistent with the importance of your A and B items?
- Are you carrying inventory quantities in excess of your maximum levels?

The first step in gaining total control over your inventory is to rank the items into A, B, C, D, E popularity codes. The old-fashioned inventory consultants will tell you that the proper way of classifying your inventory is by cost of goods sold. Multiply the units sold times the cost, which will tell you the revenue at cost generated for that item. Repeat this formula for every item, and then sort them on descending revenue (sales at cost). The top revenue producers will be at the top of the list, and the low revenue producers at the bottom. Using this method, the top X% of your items are A's, the next X% B's, etc. This is an example of how this works:

HOW TO CLASSIFY		
Cost of Item x Annual Usage	=	Sales at Cost
$10.00 x 100	=	$1,000
$15.00 x 50	=	750

In the following examples of ten items, notice the quantity sold and the cost of the items. If you rank the items on sales at cost, you will see that Items 7 and 9 are A's and Items 6 and 2 are the E's. However, if you rank the items by units, then Items 6 and 2 are the A's (they were E's based on cost of goods sold.)

ITEM #	COST	UNITS SOLD	SALES AT COST
1	$10.00	100	$1,000
2	.20	650	130
3	5.00	110	550
4	3.40	75	255
5	2.00	310	620
6	.10	800	80
7	6.75	300	2,025
8	.90	200	180
9	87.50	20	1,750
10	1.00	400	400

ITEM CLASS	SALES AT COST METHOD	UNITS METHOD
A	7	6
A	9	2
B	1	10
B	5	5
C	3	7
C	10	8
D	4	3
D	8	1
E	2	4
E	6	9

I originally used the sales at cost method until a client said; "This doesn't work. I need to classify by units because the 10-cent item that I sell every day is an A. It's not an E." You can see that neither method is correct. This is why I developed a method I call cost pools.

CLASSIFY USING COST POOLS			
ITEM COST	CLASS	ITEM #	SALES AT COST
$.01 - $2.00	A	5	$ 620
	A	10	400
	B	8	180
	B	2	130
	C	6	80
$2.01 - $10.00	A	7	$2,025
	A	1	1,000
	B	3	550
	B	4	255

Cost pools are created by ranking items of similar cost together. For example, all items that cost between $.01 and $2.00 are grouped together, $2.01 - $4.00 together, etc. You are now comparing apples with apples. I developed this method to eliminate the inequities that result from classifying sales at cost where one item costs a dollar and another costs $200. Cost pools will vary by company. I have found that breaking your inventory into eight to ten cost pools works best. If you stock 10,000 items, then each cost pool will have approximately 500 to 1500 items in it.

Pool	Cost Range		Classify Using
1	$ .01 - $	2.00	Units
2	2.01 -	4.00	Sales at Cost
3	4.01 -	8.00	Sales at Cost
4	8.01 -	16.00	Sales at Cost
5	16.01 -	32.00	Sales at Cost
6	32.01 -	64.00	Sales at Cost
7	64.01 -	128.00	Sales at Cost
8	128.01 -	99,999.00	Units

For the first cost pool and the last cost pool, you should use units. In the first pool, if you had a five-cent item and a $2.00 item, you would have to sell 40 of the five-cent item to equal the revenue generated by one of the $2.00 items. The same condition could apply to the last cost pool. Therefore, be sure to use units for the first and last pools. In pools 2 through 7, the higher cost is double the lower cost (i.e., $4.01 - $8.00). Since you never have to sell more than twice as many of the low cost items for the revenues to be equal, you should use sales at cost for pools 2 through 7.

With these cost pools, you can now properly classify like items by number of units sold from warehouse stock. I recommend that you classify the top 5 percent of your items as A. These items rank highest from a revenue-generating standpoint. The next 10 percent should be B items. A's and B's will typically account for 70 to 90 percent of your sales. The next 25 percent of the items will be C, or customer convenience items, which may not sell regularly, but you carry them as a convenience for your customers. The next 30 percent should be ranked D, and the final 30 percent E. The chart below illustrates what percentage of your items will yield what percentage of your sales. This is verified by a rank list that will be discussed in detail later.

		Cumulative %	% of Sales
Top 5%	= A	5	70
Next 10 %	= B	15	90
3rd 25 %	= C	40	96
4th 30%	= D	70	99
Bottom 30%	= E	100	100

Inventory Control

We are now going to discuss the two most important aspects of inventory control:

When should you buy an item?
(ROP, or Reorder Point)

How many should you buy?
(EOQ, or Economic Order Quantity)

These two numbers are required for automated purchasing.

A number of elements are important in calculating reorder point. We will review each one and explain how to make your reorder point as accurate as "humanly and computerly" possible.

First of all, before saying, "I can't use ROP because..." let's qualify "humanly and computerly." A good inventory system can accurately calculate ROP on 80 to 90 percent of your items. Ten to twenty percent of your inventory is made up of trouble items that need to be identified and handled by your purchasing agent on an exception basis.

The six major types of trouble items are:

1. The one time non-recurring demand, or special orders, caused by a number of situations. Identify these types of sales and, if at all possible, do not put them into your monthly usage for forecasting.

2. The majority of sales of one item on a non-monthly basis can be attributed to a single customer. For example, if you sell 75 widgets every three to four months, your reorder point will be calculated much lower than 75 and you will never have the right amount of stock to fill the order of 75.

3. The slow, sporadically moving item. Usage is 1, 0, 0, 1, 0, 2. The reorder point is either 1 or 0. Whether or not you stock one depends on your strategy.

4. Service and repair items that do not conform to sales trends.

5. Protected stock, wherein you guarantee to stock a certain item at a specified level for a customer.

6. New items.

Once you identify and handle the problem items, you can calculate accurate ROPs on the other 80 to 90%. Even the items that cause problems could be purchased automatically using some artificial intelligence.

The first integral aspect of an ROP calculation is forecasting **Average Monthly Usage (AMU)**. The most recent four to six month's history is the most important data in calculating AMU for a non-seasonal item. Remember to include sales from warehouse stock as usage figures for history, but do not include direct shipments unless you were out of stock.

For a non-seasonal item, the best projection of what you are going to sell next month is determined by what you sold in the immediate past. If you sold approximately 75 a month for each of the last six months, you would project sales of 75 next month (all things being equal). For a seasonal item, you may want to select the history of last year's activity for upcoming months' usage. Three to four months' sales history to compute the average is normally recommended.

So, by using the proper sales history from warehouse stock, and excluding large non-recurring orders, your AMU is as accurate as possible. The computer can also determine if an item's movement is consistent or in an increasing or decreasing usage trend. Based on this information, an AMU times a factor will forecast the next month's sales.

The next crucial element used to calculate ROP for an item is **Lead Time (LT)**: How many days does it take from the time you order merchandise until the time you receive it?

For starters, you may go in to your computer record by vendor and put in an estimated lead time for each vendor. Lead times change within vendors, however, and some items take longer than others to receive. Thus, for your lead time to remain as accurate as possible, your computer software system should automatically calculate lead time by item upon receipt of each new purchase order.

The ideal ROP (Re-order Point) formula is:

ROP = AMU x <u>Lead Time</u>
28 days

For example, if AMU = 100 and LT = 14 days:

ROP = 100 x <u>14</u>
28
or

ROP = 50

This means that if you sell 100 widgets per month, and it takes 14 days to receive them from your vendor, you should reorder when your stock reaches 50. When you sell the last one, the truck will be arriving at your dock to replenish the stock. Have you ever heard of J.I.T. (Just In Time)? As a distributor, you don't deal in J.I.T.; you deal in J.I.C. (Just In Case).

For a manufacturer, J.I.T. works fine. However, since your customers do not reorder in average monthly usage and the shipment may be delayed a day or more, you stand a good chance of running out of stock. Therefore, you must add another element, **Safety Stock Percent (SS%),** to this ROP formula.

The enhanced ROP formula now reads:

$$ROP = \frac{(AMU \times LT)}{28} (1 + SS\%)$$

In most industries, a safety stock percentage of 35 to 50 percent, when added to the above calculation, will yield a 96 to 98 percent service level. This will depend on the consistency of movement of the product. If you sell 100 per month like clockwork, with consistent lead time, then a safety stock of 50% may be overkill.

For example, adding a safety stock percentage of 50 percent to our original example (AMU = 100, LT = 14), our ROP equation now reads:

$$ROP = \frac{(100 \times 14)}{28} \times 1.5 = 50 \times 1.5$$

or

$$ROP = 75$$

If you have any kind of sporadic usage, this is probably your best ROP.

Another added dimension to the standard formula is the ability to vary safety stock by ABCDE code. You may want to carry a 50 percent safety stock on A items and 35 percent on C items. This method gives you the most profitable return on inventory investment by putting inventory dollars in items that turn and yield higher revenues. Your service level on C items may be slightly lower than on A's and B's.

<u>ROP with 50% Safety Stock</u>

ROP for A items: $\dfrac{(100 \times 14)}{28} (1.50) = 75$

<u>ROP with 35% Safety Stock:</u>

ROP for C items: $\dfrac{(100 \times 14)}{28} (1.35) = 65$

Carrying a 50% safety stock on C items is acceptable as long as you can demand a higher gross profit on C items. This is referred to as velocity pricing, which will help your Gross Margin Return On Investment (or turn and earn) be where it needs to be. After all, you are carrying those C items as a customer convenience - why give them away? In most cases, the customer is happy you have them and will pay a slightly higher price.

If your sales of an item are consistent (100 every month) with a variance in any month of no more than 10%, then you may need very little safety stock. If, however, the variance in demand (sporadic usage) is large, a safety stock of 60% may be needed for a 95+% fill rate.

Another method of calculating the reorder point would be to "dial-in" a desired fill rate for A, B, and C items and have the computer calculate the safety stock. This calculation will be based on the standard deviation (or probability of meeting that fill rate), considering the consistency of the monthly sales pattern for that item.

The Re-order Point formula is as accurate as "humanly and computerly" possible. It works well if you review this vendor at least once a week and there is no economic advantage to placing larger orders.

Another factor that should be considered is **Vendor Review Time (VRT),** or how often you can place a stock order to meet vendor minimums. To determine how often you can meet vendor minimums, calculate the total pounds and/or dollars you order annually from that vendor. Divide this number by the vendor's minimum order requirement. This will tell you how many times a year you could order and meet minimums. If this formula does not yield a frequent enough order cycle to reach discount or freight requirements, then you should be ordering weekly from this vendor. Doing so will increase your turns on this vendor, and the lower inventory carrying cost you incur may far exceed the 5 percent discount or prepaid freight this vendor is offering.

The formula to determine the proper buying cycle for a vendor is:

$$\frac{\text{Annual Purchases}}{\text{Economic Consideration}} = \frac{\text{No. of Times Per Year}}{\text{to Place Stock Orders}}$$

For example,

$$\frac{\$100,000 \text{ Annual Purchases}}{\begin{array}{c}\$5,000 \text{ minimum order for a } 5\% \\ \text{discount or prepaid freight}\end{array}} = \begin{array}{c}20 \text{ times per year} = \\ \text{Every 18 days}\end{array}$$

Therefore, approximately 20 orders each year will make each order the correct size to meet the minimum for this vendor. You should review this vendor approximately every 18 days. If you order more frequently, you put yourself in an excess stock position and you may destroy the next scheduled stock order. If you try to order $5,000 every week, you will have to purchase $260,000 (52 weeks x $5,000) but only sell $100,000 at cost.

You need to perform this calculation at least once a year (twice if seasonal) because variables such as the cost of money or volume with a particular vendor could change. This analysis will help you better determine which vendors you should review on a cyclical basis and which vendors may not lend themselves to that type of purchasing. The analysis illustrates that the economic consideration or freight prepaid methods are not necessarily the most profitable ways for you to buy, or possibly you are buying from the wrong vendor.

In the following example, the ROP calculated on an average monthly usage of 100, a 14 day lead time, and 50% safety stock is 75. If you review the vendor on the first of the month, the item illustrated would not be ordered because the reorder point of 75 is less than the available of 80. You have 23 days of stock on hand at an average daily usage of 3.5. The next time you can get a stock buy of $5,000 (vendor minimum) is about the 18th of the month. Your system will order this item on the next review; however, you only have five days of stock left with a 14 day lead time. The items ordered on the 18th will not be in until the 1st of the following month. You have a good probability of running out of stock.

AMU = 100   SS = 50%   LT = 14 Days   ROP = 75
Average Daily Usage = 3.5   Vendor Review Cycle = 18 days

Date	Available	Action	Days On-Hand
*1st	80	Don't Order	23
*18th	17	Order	5
23rd	0	Out of Stock	0
1st	Order Qty.	Receive	Order Qty.

Possible Lost Sales = 31 units or 9 days out of stock

*Review vendor

Remember from an earlier section that you do not want to run out of stock on an A or B item (or any item, if you can help it). Therefore, you must take Vendor Review Time (VRT) into account when calculating the ROP if you are reviewing this vendor on a cyclical basis due to economic considerations. The vendor review time has the same effect on your stocking level as lead time.

Enhancing the ROP formula to include the vendor review cycle, the formula now reads:

$$ROP = \frac{(AMU \times LT)}{28}(1 + SS\%) + \frac{(AMU \times VRT)}{28}$$

where VRT = Vendor Review Time

Unfortunately, if you review vendors on a cyclical basis, you must carry extra stock to accommodate the method of buying that you have elected. Would you carry extra stock for a D or E item? This is not likely. Similarly, you may want to carry 30 days extra stock on an A item, and only 20 days on a C item, but that would affect your service level. If an item is worth carrying and you want a high fill rate on C's, then you will need a higher margin to support the low turns.

The flexibility of varying your Vendor Review Time by ABCDE code gives you the inventory management tools to optimize your turns and profits, and control serviceability. For example, if VRT = 18 days for items on which you want to carry a 50 percent safety stock, the equation would be:

$$ROP = \frac{(100 \times 14)}{28}(1.50) + \frac{(100 \times 18)}{28}$$

or

$$ROP = 140$$

This includes the stock required to account for your vendor review cycle of buying from the vendor every 18 days to meet vendor minimum. If you have very short lead times (less than three days) and you buy the vendor twice a week, your reorder point could be too low. Make sure the combination of lead time and vendor review time is at least ten days.

The example below shows the different reorder points (ROPs) depending on the lead time and how often you can review the vendor. Based on the same sales of 100 per month, the ROP varies from 63 to 250. Each ROP is correct for a sales forecast of 100 units per month.

Item 1234
AMU = 100

Vendor	Class	Lead Time	SS%	VRT	MIN (ROP)
1	A	7	50%	7	63
2	A	14	50%	28	175
3	A	14	50%	14	125
4	A	14	50%	7	100
5	A	21	50%	28	213
6	A	28	50%	28	250

Now you can see why choosing the best strategic vendor is so important. If a vendor has long lead times and large minimum orders, your cost of doing business with that vendor is much higher. You will need to carry 3-4 times more stock in order to provide the same sales and service level to your customer.

Once again, the vendor's lead time and minimum order requirement will affect your inventory investment significantly. You would have to carry almost 400% more inventory if you bought from Vendor 6 instead of Vendor 1, and you wouldn't receive any additional revenue, gross profit dollars, or fill rate.

We have discussed when to buy and how a vendor's shipping performance and minimum requirements can affect your stock level or ROP. The next thing you need to calculate is how many to buy.

How many you should buy is determined by your **Economic Order Quantity (EOQ)**. To determine that amount, use this formula:

$$EOQ = \sqrt{\frac{24 \times \text{Cost of Ordering} \times \text{AMU}}{\text{Cost of Carrying Percent} \times \text{Unit Cost}}}$$

It costs you money to order an item and then it costs you additional money to keep it on the shelf. These costs are known as the cost of ordering and the cost of carrying inventory (incoming and outgoing costs). Before you can calculate EOQ, you must know or approximate these values.

For most distributors, the cost to order a line item on a purchase order is between $1.00 and $3.00. The cost of carrying inventory is between 25 percent and 35 percent (or 20% plus prime as a rule of thumb). If you want to be more exact you can figure your cost using the following worksheets.

INVENTORY CARRYING COST WORKSHEET

WAREHOUSE SPACE $_____
   The annual expense of warehouse in your company.
   If all your space is owned, then use the cost you'd
   expect to pay to lease equivalent space in your locale.

INSURANCE $_____
   Insurance premiums for the warehouse space and inventory.

MATERIAL HANDLING $_____
   The total annual expense in labor and material handling
   equipment (lift trucks, etc.) needed to receive and put away
   all incoming merchandise or to move it around during the
   year. (Customer order-filling expense is not included.)

TAXES $_____
   Actual taxes paid in the last fiscal year on your inventory
   and the warehouse space.

OBSOLESCENCE/SHRINKAGE $_____
   How much inventory value was written-off at the end of last
   year ... either because your physical inventory count came out
   short or certain materials were determined to be non-salable?

COST OF MONEY $_____
   Your current interest rate for borrowing money (whether
   you actually borrowed or not) applied to average value of the
   inventory throughout the year.

TOTAL COSTS $_____

Total Costs_____ $_____   =_____%
Average Inventory Value $

The answer represents your cost for carrying $1 of inventory for a year.
Acceptable range of answers: 25% to 35%.

COST OF ORDERING WORKSHEET

Total annual expense of setting-up and maintaining
records of stock on hand. (This includes the cost of all
personnel, office space, telephones, supplies, computer
time, etc.) $_____

Annual cost to expedite stock merchandise $_____

Amount of the Purchasing Department's annual expense
expended on purchase orders for stock merchandise.
(Again, this includes the personnel costs, office space,
long-distance calls, computer time, etc.) $_____

The fixed portion of the Receiving Department's annual
costs devoted to receiving and put away $_____

Amount of the Accounts Payable Department's annual
expenses devoted to processing invoices for stock merchandise.
This should be about 70% of the total cost of the department
(people, office space, supplies, computer time) $_____

TOTAL COST IN THESE CATEGORIES $_____

1. Number of purchase orders issued for stock
   merchandise in a full year   _____

2. Average number of line items on a purchase order
   for stock items   _____

   Total lines ordered in a year (No. 1 x No. 2)   _____

Calculation: <u>Total Ordering Costs</u> $_____   = $_____
                       Total Lines Ordered   **Cost to Order**

Your answer represents the number of dollars you will spend in your company
each time you go through the ordering cycle on one stock item. Acceptable
range of answers = 75 cents to $3.00 to place a single line on a purchase order.

The EOQ formula takes into consideration all the costs, along with the usage of an item, to arrive at the purchase quantity that will minimize costs and maximize the net profit. If you purchase the economic order quantity produced by the formula, each item will carry the lowest possible accumulated costs as it moves out of your warehouse. EOQ will also offer you a good turn rate.

In the example below, the EOQ for this item is 490 or a 5 month supply, based on the usage, cost of the item, and your incoming and outgoing cost (a $49 investment).

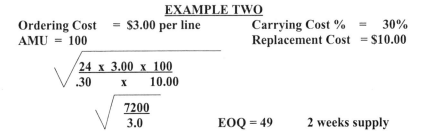

EXAMPLE ONE

Ordering Cost   = **$3.00 per line**   **Carrying Cost %**   =   **30%**
AMU = 100   **Replacement Cost**   = **$0.10**

$$\sqrt{\frac{24 \times 3.00 \times 100}{.30 \times .10}}$$

$$\sqrt{\frac{7200}{.03}} \qquad \textbf{EOQ = 490} \qquad \textbf{5 months supply}$$

With all things being equal except the item cost, which is $10.00, in the example below the system recommends an EOQ of 49, which is a two week supply or a $490 investment.

EXAMPLE TWO

Ordering Cost   = **$3.00 per line**   **Carrying Cost %**   =   **30%**
AMU = 100   **Replacement Cost**   = **$10.00**

$$\sqrt{\frac{24 \times 3.00 \times 100}{.30 \times 10.00}}$$

$$\sqrt{\frac{7200}{3.0}} \qquad \textbf{EOQ = 49} \qquad \textbf{2 weeks supply}$$

Buyers who are not using an automated system may routinely buy a one month supply, which is probably not the most economical amount to purchase.

Now it's time to buy. Since we have established the ROP and EOQ and how often we are going to review the vendor, reviewing the vendor for purchasing should be simple.

The method most adaptable to the distributor may be an **On-line Automatic Review (OAR).** Using this method, the buyer tells the purchase order program that he wants to review or create a purchase order for a specific vendor. The buyer directs the program to bring up the suggested order quantity for anything below ROP. The system automatically displays the items below reorder point and suggests the amount to order (in the proper carton or package quantity), based on your available balance, to bring your stock to the maximum level (Maximum = ROP + EOQ).

As each page of the OAR is completed, a running total of the purchase order value and weight or cubes is displayed. Upon completion of the vendor review, if you are not ordering to reach a desired weight, cube, or dollar amount, you are finished with the OAR.

If you need additional weight or dollars to complete your order, tell the OAR to order anything within X percent of reorder point (for example, 10 percent on A or B items only). Page through these screens until you reach the amount needed to meet the vendor's minimum. This method will order your most popular items that are near ROP.

Another method is to review the lines already purchased and increase the suggested quantity on specific items. This will put you in an excess stock position, so make sure you only increase fast movers.

An On-line Automatic Review can also be run at night for any number of vendors. In the morning, your buyer can review the purchase orders before they are automatically faxed or sent via EDI to your vendor. If you are not close to your vendor minimums after the review of the vendor, the purchase order should be deleted and the vendor reviewed at a later date.

Remember my client who has 30,000 items and 7 branches with a central warehouse? To complicate matters, he has three different businesses in one: appliance parts, building maintenance products, and heating and air conditioning, which is seasonal in his area. He has eight branches with walk-in trade (contractors) and retail counters.

He has reengineered the purchasing part of the pro-curement process. Every month his inventory is automatically classified into A, B, C, D, and E items. His Re-order Points and Economic Order Quantities are recalculated using accurate data. Because of this, his computer can review any number of vendors nightly, determine if a suggested purchase order is near the vendor's minimum requirements, check all branches for excess or shortages, and let the buyer review what it did. The buyer approves, modifies, or deletes the purchase order. It then is EDIed or digitally faxed to the vendor. I call this reengineered process "PO Autobuy."

So, if you say, "I am different; it will not work for me," then you are not ready, willing, or able to consider reengineering your business. But if you are, just think of the payback.

Inventory Management

It is not enough to focus solely on knowing when and how many to buy. It is necessary to manage your inventory as well, which will reduce excess stock and significantly improve your profit picture. You can then apply more funds toward working inventory, which will allow you to provide the service levels your customers require. Inventory Management also focuses on improving GMROI (Gross Margin Return On Investment).

Are you getting an acceptable return? If you had $50,000, what would you do with it? Would you invest it in bonds? Would you invest in the stock market? Would you go to Las Vegas and put it on "red"? Or would you invest it in inventory? As a distributor, you have elected to invest it in inventory. Are you getting a return on your investment?

Go into your warehouse and look at specific aisles and shelves, and say to yourself, "That section right there represents $50,000. There's $150,000 down that aisle; and over there, there's $75,000." You are looking at three different investments - three product groups or three vendors. Do you know what your return is on each investment? If you don't, then you do not have a handle on your assets.

Imagine that you gave $2 million to an investment firm, who invested various amounts of your money into 60 different stocks. At the end of the year they told you, "Your return on investment for everything was 8.3 percent. However, we don't have any idea which investments were at 15 percent, and which were at zero." You would fire them immediately! What kind of business investors could not tell their clients which investments to drop and which to increase? Many distributors are unaware of which products (investments) to drop because they don't track the true return on their investment (inventory).

An excellent method of analyzing your investment in inventory is an Inventory Analysis Report that shows Gross Margin Return On Investment (GMROI) by product category and by total inventory investment. A desirable range is between 1.3 and 4.0. If it's less than 1.3, you are not getting a good return on your investment. If it's greater than 4.0, you probably do not have enough inventory. If you had more, you could probably sell more. Take a close look at your fill rate for any line which is 4.0 or greater.

A tool my clients use is an Inventory Analysis Report, which is the best means to evaluate and track the use of assets committed to inventory. You should be aware of:

1. return on the investment in inventory
2. true return on investment (less non-stock items)
3. what product groups are most productive
4. how much inventory is needed
5. what items are not needed
6. what your fill rate is
7. how to correct or adjust any of the above

Following is a page from a sample Inventory Analysis Report. The report will show how each product group is performing. The totals at the end of the report will show you exactly how your business is doing. The numbers on which you want to focus are GMROI, Excess Stock, and Service Level.

```
15.2*1696=/98  11:18AM        I N V E N T O R Y   A N A L Y S I S           INANLYSIS Version U7.60.00   PAGE   3
PROGRAM OPTIONS:1;1;6;IN01;IN02;N;N;Y;*
MONTH ENTERED: 6
CATEGORY/CLASS:IN02   INDUSTRIAL                  SERVICE CODE: ALL
```

PART NUMBER	LOC	DESCRIPTION	CLASS	ON HAND	RSV	PFLG	MAX	LAST SALE	INVENTORY VALUE	YTD UNITS	YTD COST	YTD PROFIT	GP%	TURN	GMROI	MTD SVC	YTD SVC
56789	1	INSET CNGA 643T	A	246			277	3/98	3793	1696	26154	10264	28.2	13.79	5.41	98.3	97.9
80989	1	MATRIX 14'3X1X.035	A	34			119	3/98	1275	172	6463	2419	27.2	10.14	3.79	95.4	96.9
69957306636	1	BELT 25X48 180G R823	A	89			144	8/98	1954	677	14874	7568	33.7	15.22	7.75	97.2	97.8
43160	1	BRUSH 8-03	A	75			131	6/98	1944	770	19967	9667	32.6	20.54	9.95	97.5	98.1
13195	1	TAP 5/8-11 H3 3FL GUN	A	268 *			19	1/98	3564	1844	24523	8530	25.8	13.76	4.79	96.9	97.4
66141133130	1	DISC ROLL 6" 180G STK	A	74			125	8/98	3248	223	9804	3522	26.4	6.04	2.17	98.4	98.7
46382	1	TOOL HOLDER VHM 20109	A	178 *			141	7/98	7431	489	20416	8198	28.7	5.49	2.21	99.4	98.9
ZZIN02N	1		N	0		1			0	1	0	0	0.0	.00	.00		

```
**TOTALS FOR CATEGORY/CLASS IN02       EXCESS $  4781       T & E
                                                            306.42    23209         122201   50168   29.1  10.53   4.32    97.6  98.0

**TOTALS FOR CLASSIFICATION
                                   A              4781       306.42    23209         122201   50168   29.1  10.53   4.32    97.6  98.0
                                   B                           .00        0              0       0    0.0    .00    .00
                                   C                           .00        0              0       0    0.0    .00    .00
                                   D                           .00        0              0       0    0.0    .00    .00
                                   E                           .00        0              0       0    0.0    .00    .00
                                   N                           .00        0              0       0    0.0    .00    .00
                                   Z                           .00        0              0       0    0.0    .00    .00
```

The Inventory Analysis is designed to summarize use of assets committed to inventory. When viewed as a score sheet, it becomes a valuable tool in tracking progress toward more efficient management of assets. The report records information by the item, subtotals to category/class, and summarizes totals for inventory. The result is a method to track the goals of sales and purchasing on one document. The numbers that follow summarize uses of assets tied to inventory.

A. EXCESS

Excess inventory occurs when an item's available-for-sale is greater than its maximum.

> Available (On hand less demand)
> -   Maximum (Reorder point + EOQ)
> = Excess

This calculation is made for each line item. An asterisk appears to the right of on-hand for all line items where available is greater than maximum. Excess quantities multiplied by the cost per item are totaled by A, B, C, D, E, N, and Z classifications by category/class and for the entire inventory.

The EXCESS $ on the sample Inventory Analysis Report are dollars not justified by sales history, safety stock, or reserve stock. By definition, they are excess inventory. Excess inventory in A and B classifications is less a problem than in C, D, or E, because these items have a better chance of selling. To have a consistent evaluation of inventory, it is important to reclassify your inventory every thirty days.

B. T & E (TURN AND EARN)

The intent of T & E is to compare the profitability of low-turn, high-margin items with high-turn, low-margin items. Many distributors mislead themselves by believing either that low margins are justified by selling more, or that high margins are profitable despite low volume.

These assumptions are true provided the margins are complemented by appropriate turns. A rule of thumb is a minimum T & E of 100. The examples below indicate variations of movement and margin. All of them end with the same T & E.

T & E	=	TURNS	X	GROSS MARGIN
100	=	2	X	50%
100	=	4	X	25%
100	=	10	X	10%

C. AVERAGE INVENTORY VALUE

The average inventory value is calculated by multiplying the average on-hand for the past 12 months times the average cost.

D. YTD COST (COST OF GOODS SOLD)

The YTD Cost of Goods Sold is calculated by multiplying the units sold times the average cost.

E. YTD PROFIT (GROSS MARGIN)

YTD Gross Margin is calculated by subtracting the YTD sales from the YTD cost.

F. GP% (GROSS PROFIT PERCENTAGE)

Gross Profit Percentage is calculated for each item record by dividing gross margin dollars by the sum of cost of goods sold plus gross margin. The category/class subtotal and total GP% are calculated from item record totals of CGS (Cost of Goods Sold) and GM$ (Gross Margin Dollars).

G. TURNS

Traditionally, a distributor measured his asset management performance by how many times he turned his inventory. Because cost of goods sold grows throughout a fiscal year, it must be annualized before it is compared to inventory. Many distributors use this method to calculate turns:

$$\text{TURNS} = \frac{\text{YTD Cost X (12/Current Month)}}{\text{Average Inventory}}$$

This calculation inflates turns. True turns are calculated by removing inventory and Cost of Goods Sold associated with non-stock and/or direct sales. The calculation for turns is:

Gross Sales	$ 4,000,000
- Gross Margin	- 1,000,000
= Cost of Goods Before Directs	= 3,000,000
- Direct Shipments	- 600,000
= Cost of Goods From Stock	= 2,400,000
/ Inventory	/ 800,000
= Turns	= 3 Turns

H. GMROI (Gross Margin Return On Investment)

GMROI is calculated by annualizing YTD profit and dividing by inventory.

$$\frac{\text{\$ YTD Profit X (12/Month)}}{\text{\$ Inventory}}$$

I. Service Level

This is the number of stock lines shipped complete and on time divided by the number of stock lines ordered. If an item was ordered 20 times and shipped complete by the customer request date 19 times, then your fill rate is 95% for that item. The monthly analysis reports your fill rate by product class by vendor for A through E. The goal of inventory management is to attain a 96-98% fill rate with a profitable GMROI and as little excess stock as possible. Remember, you cannot manage what you cannot measure.

Another tool, called the "Product Rank Analysis Report," will show you what percentage of your inventory makes up what percentage of your sales. Go to the Cumulative Percent of Sales column, find the items that make up 98% of your sales, draw a line, and everything below that line is your dead stock program. Make them non-stock items and get rid of them. (You make them non-stock so you do not buy them again.)

```
DATE  7/06/98  11:17AM          P R O D U C T   R A N K   A N A L Y S I S   R E P O R T      INRANKLST Version U7.60.00  PAGE  1
PROGRAM OPTIONS:S;Y;*;Y;Y;A;N;PH01;PH02;1;*
TOTAL SALES:    $151,844          TOTAL INVENTORY:    $30,334          TOTAL ITEMS:    63
```

PART NUMBER	LOC	ITEM COUNT	PCT ITEMS	UNIT COST		SALES AT COST	CUM SALES AT COST	CUM PCT SALES	DOLLAR INVENTORY	CUM DOLLARS INVENTORY	CUM PCT INVENTORY	UNIT SALES	CLASS
328-2224	1	1	1.6	15.420	E	26,154	26,154	17.2	3,793	3,793	12.5	1696	A
75/8' WEIL MCLAIN HEAT ELEM ONLY													
271-2126	1	2	3.2	13.300	E	24,523	50,677	33.4	3,564	7,357	24.3	1844	A
821 W 24X6 SIDEWALL SPLY													
LKD23322-4	1	3	4.8	41.780	E	20,416	71,093	46.8	7,431	14,788	48.8	489	A
ELKAY D23322 4 HOLE DOUBLE SINK													
ZN415-5B3NH	1	4	6.3	25.920	E	19,967	91,060	60.0	1,944	16,732	55.2	770	B
ZURN ZN415-5B 3" NH FLOOR DRAIN													
731-2696	1	5	7.9	21.950	E	14,874	105,934	69.8	1,954	18,686	61.6	677	B
SCRW D&T 10-16X1/2 500 PAK													
2385.400-002	1	6	9.5	43.890	E	9,804	115,738	76.2	3,248	21,934	72.3	223	B
AS2385.400 CHR LAV FAUCET													
235-3065	1	7	11.1	37.500	E	6,464	122,201	80.5	1,275	23,209	76.5	172	B
1127-2 STRAP ON AQUA STAT													

I remember the first time one of my clients ran their rank list and found out that 99% of their sales was made up of 52% of their 12,000 SKUs (items). "How can this be?" the owner asked. The office manager proceeded to tell him, "You let any salesperson tell the buyers to add products to the inventory so they can cater to a new customer." Needless to say, that policy changed quickly. One of the most important decisions a distributor has to make is what he should stock. This distributor should never have allowed a salesperson to add products to the inventory as stock items to serve one customer with no commitment. What is stocked is a decision that should be made by management.

The Procurement Process Summary

1. Establish strong vendor relationships with technology-oriented vendors that can provide you bar coded items with short lead times and low minimum requirements. Be prepared to communicate with the vendor via EDI, eliminating the need for costly paper transactions that require input and are susceptible to errors.
2. Since your computer knows virtually every bit of information about an item, such as its usage pattern, lead times, safety stock, costs, history, classification, order frequency and fill rate, have it calculate a reorder point and economic order quantity every month on the majority of the items.
3. Have the computer review all vendors on a regular schedule and automatically create the optimum purchase order in carton quantity. These purchase orders can be easily re-

worked, edited, and EDIed to your vendor. The vendor will confirm ship dates and prices automatically via EDI.

4. Utilize the suggested inventory management tools to manage your assets, track fill rates, reduce excess stock, and improve your return on investment.

5. With all things being equal, if you simply increase your turns by two-tenths of a turn per year for five years (one turn), you will double your bottom line profits.

4

THE WAREHOUSING PROCESS

To date, the warehouse is probably the most neglected area of the small to medium sized distributor. Reengineering the warehousing process will yield tremendous savings by increasing productivity and count accuracy, and by reducing errors.

Whenever I am talking to distributors about inventory, I discuss three critical areas:

1. Stock Status
2. Inventory Control
3. Inventory Management

We have already discussed inventory control (ROPs and EOQs) and inventory management (Inventory Analysis and Inventory Rank List). You can't effectively accomplish either without stock status. Stock status means at least 99% accuracy from shelf to computer record. If the computer says you have 10 but you cannot locate them, your service and productivity will suffer. You cannot sell what you cannot find.

Cycle Counting

The best advice I have for distributors who need to cycle count is to stop doing it. It's synonymous to mopping up the floor every day instead of fixing the leak. If you receive 100% accurately and you pick 100% accurately, then why do you need to cycle count?

There is no way, however, that you can eliminate the need for cycle counting if you continue to receive or pick manually with a minimum wage worker, if you refuse to automate and bar code, or if your vendor does not ship with a high degree of accuracy. If you do not track your vendor's performance, you will not know what he is costing you in errors.

Remember, you will need to ask yourself the following questions: Do my products come in bar-coded? If so, is the bar code readable and identifiable in my system?

If the vendor does not bar code the product, then you must consider alternate methods of receiving, and applying internal bar codes.

Radio Frequency Bar Code Terminals

The reengineered warehousing process of receiving, stocking, and picking *must* include real time Radio Frequency Terminals capable of reading bar codes. Today's technology is affordable, and the payback can be seen in a year or less.

There are several different methods of receiving. The method(s) you choose will depend on whether your vendor bar codes the items or not. Receiving methods will also vary depending on the size of the items, and how they are packaged.

Remember, just because the product comes in bar-coded does not mean you are home free. Your computer must be able to cross reference the bar code identifier to your Item Master record. If the UPC code for an item is 18632-01763, and your computer uses your part number "A37," you must build a link between the bar code identifier and your item number identifier. The easiest way is if you are using the vendor's part number as your part number and he provides you with a diskette of the cross-references of his number to the UPC number (Do not count on this!). The most productive way to build this link is for your RF (Radio Frequency) terminal to have an Inquiry look up by your part number (or you can key in your part number). When you scan the bar code, it will automatically build a permanent link. Then every time you receive, move, or pick that item by scanning it, the system will know with which item you are dealing.

5

RECEIVING

If your vendor bar codes, the boxes that have just been unloaded may have a shipping label with a PO identifier on each of them. If so, you can scan the POs that you are receiving. The RF unit will instantly verify that the PO is valid in your system. If your supplier does not provide your PO number bar coded, you will have to remove the packing slips and enter the PO or POs on this shipment. As an alternative to finding the box with the packing slip, you should be able to scan an item. If there is only one open PO for that item, your computer will know what PO was just received. If there is more than one open PO for that item, the system will suggest that you scan another item. This is helpful if you are unloading a semi and you want to start receiving as soon as you unload, but you have not yet unloaded the box with the packing slip.

Receiving can be different for each company, and developing the most efficient receiving process for your company will depend on a number of variables. Describing every one of those variables would be very confusing and very boring. I will describe the methods that are most efficient for three possibilities.

(1) Every item in this shipment is bar coded.

(2) No items are bar coded.

(3) Most items are bar coded, or most cartons are bar coded.

#1 - Every item in this shipment is bar coded.
Step 1

Scan or enter purchase order number. (Scan an item to determine PO number.)

Purchase order(s) are valid - okay to receive.

Step 2

Enter receiver number or have the system generate the receiver number using the purchase order number and the date.

Step 3

Scan the permanent bar coded number of the cart or pallet on which items will be put for the put away procedure. Consider these carts or pallets movable bins. To help simplify the put away procedure, you may want to scan a different pallet for each zone. Then, upon receiving the item, the computer can tell the receiving person on which pallet to put the received part (This works best for small parts using fixed bin location with overflow). If you are not using fixed bins or zones, this step may not provide any benefit.

Step 4

Each item is now scanned. The computer validates each scanned item as a valid part and confirms it is valid for this purchase order. The quantity is accumulated and compared to the total quantity ordered.

If an item is invalid (not a valid part or not a valid item on this PO), the system will add it to the PO as a reject and the receiving person will be instructed to put it aside.

If one or more of the items received is for a customer back order, or will be able to fill a back order, then the receiving person will be instructed to set all or a portion of those items aside as well. Otherwise, they will be put on the pallet or cart for put away by zone.

This form of receiving will be similar to a grocery store check out where each item is scanned. If items are bar coded, it will be the fastest and most accurate method.

#2 - No items are bar coded

The same process as before needs to take place. Enter the purchase order and receiver number; scan bar coded carts or pallets for put away.

The receiving person will manually enter the first 'X' characters of the item being received. The RF terminal will scroll the parts on that PO that match the characters entered. Once the item is selected, the description and quantity to be received will be displayed. The receiver will then verify the quantity received. At this time, the proper number of bar code labels will print and can be applied to the items. The same set-aside message or reject message will occur.

#3 - Most items are bar coded, or most cartons are bar coded

This is a combination of possibilities one and two. The item is scanned (because a bar code exists), but the quantity is counted and verified as in method two rather than scanning each item.

If the items received are not bar coded and you do not have fixed bin locations for items, then an identification label will need to be printed and applied to each box or item, as discussed earlier.

What have we accomplished?

At the receiving area, we have, on-line:

1. confirmed that the PO was valid before we began the receiving process
2. received all items; verified that they were valid items on the PO
3. verified the exact quantity received and alerted the receiving person or supervisor of any problems (over shipment, under shipment)
4. told the receiving person how many to set aside for customer backorders that need to be staged, shipped out immediately, or transferred to replenish a branch
5. updated the computer as to what was checked in
6. set up the vendor payment for the goods received

This was all accomplished by just scanning an item as it was unpacked or unloaded.

Changing the Old Way

In the past, you would take the packing slip and verify it with a hard copy of the PO, then you would enter the quantity received into the computer at a terminal in an office. The next step would be to send the set of documents to Accounts Payable to wait for the vendor invoice. The invoice would be checked against the PO for prices, and the packing slip (or receiving report) for quantity and then the vendor's invoice would be entered. If there was any discrepancy, the invoice would be held and returned to the buyer. The buyer then called the supplier, and they determined who was correct. In a reengineered distributor, *all* those steps and *all* the related paperwork is eliminated or streamlined, and the receiving errors are virtually eliminated.

If you EDI a purchase order to the vendor, and your prices are verified and acknowledged via EDI, you will pay him the price to which you agreed before he shipped it. You do not need the vendor's invoice because you have already verified every item and quantity received via bar coding. Only when the quantity received is incorrect do you need to contact the vendor.

Radio Frequency Procedural Flow

We have discussed methodology. Following is an example of a practical Radio Frequency System, including sample screens. The RF terminals are interactive with the computer database. Batch terminals are outdated for most distributor applications.

The PO number will be entered, scanned, or determined by scanning an item. The receiving person will select the best receiving method. If all items are bar coded, the receiver will most likely choose Options PF1 or PF2. If the items are not bar coded, Option PF3 will be used to look up parts, and labels will be printed upon receiving.

```
              RECEIVING
              ENTER PO# _____


        PF1 - SCAN AND ENTER QTY
        PF2 - SCAN ALL PARTS
        PF3 - DISPLAY PARTS
        PF4 - RETURN TO MENU
        ENTER P.O.# AND PRESS RETURN
```

The PO is validated, and the following data will be displayed. If there is more than one PO being received, additional POs can be entered.

```
        ABC VENDOR SUPPLY
        P.O.#    989    02/14/96

   ENTER ADDITIONAL PO's
   THAT ARE INCLUDED OR
   ENTER TO CONTINUE.
   P.O.#_____    ENTER
   (Can enter additional P.O.'s.)
```

On the next screen, the receiving person can scan the cart that will be used for put away for each zone. If you are using zoned put-away, the program requires a zone to be entered for each pallet.

```
        CART OR PALLET #
         *PLT01   ENTER

        ZONE A

        PF1 - PRINT LABELS
        PF3 - VOID, PF4 - END
```

If PF1 is entered, then the program will print bar code labels for each part or carton, which can be applied at receiving time. Again, this option should be used if the items received do not have bar code labels.

On the next screen, the receiving person will scan the first item.

```
ITEM# XXXXXX
P.O.#   989
ABC VENDOR SUPPLY
OPTIONS:
PF1  -   DISPLAY PARTS
PF2  -   SCAN NEW CART
PF4 -    END THIS P.O.
```

If it is not on the purchase order, the system will display the reject screen so the part can be added to the purchase order.

```
PART#  XXXXXX
IS INVALID ON THIS
P.O.  ADD THIS ITEM
TO THE P.O.?   Y/N
ITEM WILL BE HANDLED
AS REJECT.
```

If yes is chosen, the following screen will display:

```
PART# XXXXXX
PART XXXXXX  DESCRIPTION
QTY             QTY
OPEN          RECVED  U/M
                  1      EA
              PF4 - VOID
```

The item will be added to the PO as a received item, i.e., the vendor shipped you a wrong part. The part should be set aside and a return PO should be created. In the meantime, the item is accounted for and can be dealt with without being lost. Chances are if the vendor shipped it, it will probably be on his invoice. That is why you need to receive it, track it, and return it.

If the part number was entered incorrectly or if the bar code number is not set up in your system, the receiving person can look it up. Instead of handling the item as a reject, he answers "N" to add the part. He will return to this screen and then select PF1 display parts.

```
ITEM#  TEST PART
P.O.#   989
ABC VENDOR SUPPLY
 OPTIONS:
 PF1 - DISPLAY PARTS
 PF2 - SCAN NEW CART
 PF4 - END THIS P.O.
```

The display screen will start at the beginning of the purchase order or start with the part or partial part entered (TEST PART). One of the parts displayed can be selected by pressing PF1, PF2, or PF3. Pressing enter will continue displaying parts until the item is found; PF4 will stop display mode.

```
TEST PART 1 (PF1)
1/2" COPPER ELBOW
TEST PART 2 (PF2)
3/8" COPPER ELBOW
TEST PART 3 (PF3)
3/4" COPPER ELBOW
ENTER TO CONTINUE
(PF4) STOP DISPLAY
```

If the part scanned or entered is a valid part on the PO, then the system will automatically accept it and continue to the next logical screen.

The screen will display: your part number, zone (if applicable), description, manufacturer's number, purchase order quantity, and backordered quantity.

On the following screen, the option to scan all parts was chosen at the beginning; therefore, the "QTY OPEN" represents the quantity not received and the quantity received defaults to one or to the box quantity associated with that bar code. If the bar code scanned was a box label, the computer knows how many are in the box. It also tells the receiving person to set aside the item for a back order.

```
# XXXXX          ZONE A
DESC XXXXX
MFG PART XXXXX
QTY           QTY
OPEN          RECVED U/M
  10 EA           1     EA
SET ASIDE  1    B/O
PF1 - LBL  PF2 - PLT  PF3 - OPTS
```

If PF1 is pressed, the part label(s) will print immediately. If the part received is a special order, the label will include the customer PO number and ship-to and your order number, bar coded. It can then be put in a staging area until it is shipped and the computer will know where all specials are staged.

If PF2 is selected, the pallet screen will be displayed to scan the cart or pallet on which the item was put. The backordered quantity will not be put on the put-away pallet. If a pallet was already scanned for this zone or for this receiving, scanning a new pallet is not necessary unless it is full.

If PF3 is chosen, the options screen will be displayed. This screen will allow a bar code to be scanned. This bar code number will be written to the part cross-reference file. This is a method of updating the vendor's bar code number into the item file when receiving.

It will also allow the receiving person to put the item away immediately. This is helpful if receiving a pallet or a large item with a lift truck. It can be unloaded, recorded, and put away in one step.

If the option to scan and enter quantity was chosen, the quantity in the backorder column of the purchase order will show as the quantity open on this purchase order, and that quantity will be automatically entered in the quantity received. It can be overridden. In the example below, the open PO quantity is 10.

If ten are counted, the receiver will press ENTER. If he only counts five, then five will be entered into the quantity received, overriding the ten.

```
# XXXXX              ZONE B
DESCRIPTION XXXXXXX
MFG PART XXXXXX
QTY         QTY
OPEN        RECVED U/M
  10 EA         5    EA
SET ASIDE 5 B/O
PF1 - LBL  PF2 - PLT  PF3 - OPTS
```

If the quantity received was overridden earlier to five and this part was scanned again later in this receiving, the quantity open will be five. The quantity received (5) will be accepted and added to the original quantity received.

```
┌─────────────────────────────────────────┐
│ # XXXXX                    ZONE B        │
│ DESCRIPTION  XXXXXXX                      │
│ MFG PART XXXXXX                           │
│ QTY          QTY                          │
│ OPEN         RECVED U/M                   │
│  5  EA           5      EA                │
│ PF1 - LBL  PF2 -  PLT  PF3 - OPTS         │
└─────────────────────────────────────────┘
```

If the item(s) is serialized, then the next scan will be a serial number. If it is lot controlled, then the lot number and quantity will need to be entered. Serial parts will be displayed as follows:

```
┌─────────────────────────────────────────┐
│ # XXXXX                    ZONE B        │
│ DESCRIPTION XXXXX                         │
│ SER#_____                      │
│  QTY          QTY                         │
│ OPEN          RECVED U/M                  │
│  10 EA            1      EA               │
│ SET ASIDE 1 B/O                           │
│ PF1 - LBL  PF2 - PLT  PF3 - OPTS          │
└─────────────────────────────────────────┘
```

Lot numbered items received will be displayed as ENTER LOT NUMBER and the quantity received will default to quantity open.

Lot items will display as follows:

```
┌─────────────────────────────────────────┐
│  # XXXXX                    ZONE B        │
│  DESCRIPTION XXXXXX                        │
│  LOT# _____                     │
│   QTY              QTY                      │
│   OPEN             RECVED U/M               │
│   10 EA              10      EA             │
│  SET ASIDE 5 B/O                           │
│  PF1 - LBL  PF2 - PLT  PF3 - OPTS          │
└─────────────────────────────────────────┘
```

The item will be written to the put-away work file, with pallet number, part number, and quantity to be put away (only if the entire quantity is not set aside for backorders).

You can see how quickly and accurately receiving can be done if the items are bar coded and the bar codes are identifiable on your system. You will have no paper, no errors, no redundant work, no manual entry, and no delays. You simply scan the bar code and the item is received.

Filling of Back Orders - Allocation of Stock

Upon receiving an item, the computer interactively informs the receiving person as to the disposition of the item received. For example, "put 'X' number of items aside to fill customer orders or branch transfers and put the balance away." After receiving a PO or a group of POs, the receiving person can tell the computer to allocate the stock received to customer back orders. Allocation should be done on a first-come, first-served basis with override capabilities if there is not enough stock to cover all of the back orders. As part of the allocation procedure, any documents required to ship the back orders can be automatically printed. If it is a ship complete order (tag and hold), then the item may need to be staged rather than shipped. A label identifying the order number and customer should be printed and applied along with the staging area identifier. Any special order items that are received will be allocated to the customer's order.

If the vendor ships the wrong item or over-ships the item, the buyer will be notified of the rejects. If there are no errors, the payment to the vendor can be done automatically. No invoices (Ford Motor Company).

Receiving Summary

1. When getting started in the automated warehouse, the first step is to lay out your warehouse in zones with a good bin locator system and bar code the bins with the bin numbers.
2. Make sure your items are bar coded with readable bar codes. If the vendor does not bar code, make sure you print and apply labels upon receiving. Use a bar code reader to update the vendor's bar code numbers.
3. Determine which items will have fixed bins and which items will be conducive to a random locator system. Mix and match is okay.
4. Use RF spread spectrum scanning equipment to automate the receiving part of the warehouse process.

6

STOCKING (PUT AWAY)

Now that the items have been received, and allocated items have been set aside for staging or shipping, we need to begin our "put away" process.

The put away process can vary by company, by warehouse, by whether you are using a random locator system or fixed bins, or a combination of the two, and by whether you receive pallets or small items. In the item record, the computer knows if an item is fixed bin or random, and if the fixed bin is full or not (Quick Pick area).

Example 1 - Putting Away Items on a Pallet that is Bar Coded, Using Fixed Bins

A stocker (a person who puts away stock) scans the pallet number. The computer knows exactly what is on the pallet. When the receiving person checked it in and determined the disposition, he scanned the pallet on which he put it.

Upon scanning the pallet to be put away, the computer will direct the stocker to the first location to which he needs to go and tell the stocker what item he needs to put away. The stocker scans the bin location where he is and scans the item he is putting there. This will ensure that he puts the right item in the right location. If the fixed bin is full, the computer directs him to an alternate bin where the item's overflow is stocked.

If you are using fixed bins and tracking quantity per bin, the computer will know if the primary pick bin is full or needs replenishment, and will then direct the stocker to the appropriate spot.

In the event that the fixed bin is full and there are no alternate bins previously assigned, the stocker puts the item anywhere there is space. Upon scanning the bin where he put the item, the computer will update the item record with the bin and the quantity put there.

If, however, there are multiple items in a bin with no bar code labels, you are leaving yourself open to possible picking errors due to visual confirmation. That is why I recommended printing labels upon receiving to eliminate the possibility of errors if the items are not bar coded from the vendor.

Once again, the reengineered distributor will have either received the items bar coded or applied a bar code label that contained the part number or a unique license plate to each box.

Example 2 - Random Warehousing Receiving; Pallets with Same Item

One of my clients is a paint manufacturer whose warehouse receives pallets with a single SKU on each pallet. Upon receiving, the computer prints a license plate for each pallet received and knows what and how many are on each pallet. The stocker picks up the pallet, puts it anywhere in the zone where it belongs and scans the license plate to the bin location where he put it. The computer now knows exactly what is on each pallet and where the pallet is. Don't you wish your life was that simple?

Example 3 - Random Locator System; With Variable Quantities In a Box and Multiple Items on a Pallet

This method is a bit more complicated than example two, but just as easy for the stocker. Another one of my clients distributes garments. Upon receiving, the computer is told how many garments are in each box (a tally). A unique license plate is then generated for each box. The computer knows via the license plate what item and what quantity is in the box, even if the quantity varies. As the license plates are applied to each box, the box is placed on a pallet and scanned to that pallet (which has a bar code on it). The computer now knows exactly what is on each pallet (like example 2). The stocker puts the pallet anywhere and scans the bin in which he put the pallet.

My client has a 150,000 square foot warehouse under one roof, with 250,000 boxes (that all look alike) of garments, with 99.5% accuracy.

Applying a license plate to each box or item, in the event they are not bar coded, will insure accuracy and is virtually fail safe.

- The computer knows what is in each box.
- Quantities per box can vary.
- You do not need to worry about cross-reference part numbers or variable item numbers.
- Will allow for true random locator system as well as multiple items per bin or pallet.
- Can just put away pallets and not each item.
- If the items come in bar coded, you may still want a unique license plate, especially if there is a variable quantity in a box or you need to track lots.

Quick Pick or Fixed Bins

If you have small parts or loose parts, you should use a quick pick area with fixed bins for your A & B items.

The computer can keep track of the quantity each bin holds and generate a transfer from bulk to the quick pick area. In this situation, the bulk would be license plated and the quick pick may be loose parts by part number. If you are fortunate enough to have your items come in with a usable bar code and quantity per box does not vary, you can accomplish this without applying a license plate or your own bar code label. The method you use will vary depending on the vendor.

The put away process assumes you scanned the parts to a cart or pallet. This allows the computer to direct the stocker to the correct bin or zone. In the event the items received are not conducive to a cart or pallet, the stocker can scan a part and the system will direct him to the appropriate location for that item.

Below are some sample screens for the put away process with an explanation of how the stocker will function.

The following screen appears when put-away is selected from the main menu. If you are using bar coded carts or pallets, then the cart or pallet can be scanned.

```
CART / PALLET _____

PF1  - ITEM  PUT-AWAY
PF2  - PALLET BIN SEQUENCE
PF3  - PUT-AWAY ENTIRE
         PALLET IN RANDOM
         LOCATION  _____
PF4  - END
```

If PF1 - ITEM PUT-AWAY is selected, the first item to be put away will be scanned.

```
ITEM# _____


PF2 -   PALLET BIN SEQUENCE
PF3 -   PUT-AWAY ENTIRE
        PALLET IN RANDOM
        LOCATION _____
PF4 -   END
```

When the item is scanned, the following screen will be displayed, which will show the stocker the fixed bin location. When arriving at the proper location, the stocker scans the bin or part (depending on whether the fixed bin location is bar coded with the part number or the bin number), verifying that he is at the correct location.

```
ITEM#   XXXXXXXXXXXXXX
XXXXXXXXXXXXXXXXXXXXX
MFG. PART XXXXXXXXXXXX

BIN   XXXXXXX
BIN/PART _____
PF3 -   VOID
```

If a bin/part is scanned for verification and the bin/part does not match, the following screen will appear. If the stocker wants to put the item in a specific bin, he scans the bin number to update, or presses PF4 to void (in the event that he is in the wrong place).

```
ITEM#  XXXXXXXXXXXXXXX
XXXXXXXXXXXXXXXXXXXXXX
MFG. PART  XXXXXXXXXXXX

BIN    XXXXXXX
BIN/PART  YYYY
WRONG PLACE
UPDATE BIN# ____   OR PF4 - VOID
```

The stocker continues to scan and put away each item on the cart or pallet until the cart or pallet is empty.

PF2 - Pallet Bin Sequence

If this option is chosen, the program will read the pallet file in primary bin sequence and walk the stocker through the warehouse in bin location sequence. This procedure will be the same as the item put-away for verification.

```
ITEM#    XXXXXXXXXXXXXX
XXXXXXXXXXXXXXXXXXXXXX
MFG. PART  XXXXXXXXXXXX

BIN    XXXXXXX
BIN/PART        _____
PF3 -   VOID
```

If void is selected in this mode, it will return to the item entry screen. The stocker can scan or enter an item and continue in that mode until he selects PF2 to return to the pallet bin sequence mode. Only those items that have not been put away will start displaying in bin sequence. This allows the stocker to be directed through the warehouse in bin sequence. However, if the item on top is not the next suggested item, the stocker can change modes to item put away, then return to bin sequence if desired.

```
ITEM# _____



PF2 -    PALLET BIN SEQUENCE
PF3 -    PALLET PUT-AWAY
         RANDOM LOCATION
PF4 -    END
```

PF3 - Put-away Entire Pallet

Using this selection is simply moving a full pallet to a specific bin location. This will be used if the stocker wants to move an entire pallet. He will scan the pallet, and the location, and press PF3.

```
CART/PALLET _____

PF1 -    ITEM PUT-AWAY
PF2 -    PALLET BIN SEQUENCE
PF3 -    PUT AWAY ENTIRE
         PALLET IN RANDOM
         LOCATION _____
PF4 -    END
```

Put Away Summary

1. The idea essential to RF is that everything is interactive. No matter where a part is put, the computer knows where it is. If the item is to be put in a fixed bin, it will verify that the item is being put in the right place.

2. In the past, only experienced persons that knew where things went could put them away. Now, anyone can put items away correctly.
3. If you move an item, make sure its new bin location is scanned and updated.
4. The computer will know where everything is, and how many are in each warehouse location.

PICKING

The computer knows:

1. about every open order in the system
2. what stock is allocated to what order
3. when the order needs to ship (date)
4. the route/stop if applicable
5. the weight/cubes of each order
6. how it is going to be shipped
7. its picking priority in relation to all other orders in the system
8. how many trucks are available and/or needed
9. where every item is in the warehouse
10. what picker is available and if he is driving a fork lift, using a hand truck, or pushing a cart

The picker clocks in as available. The RF terminal tells him what order to pick next, and directs him to a specific location. He scans the bin to verify he is at the correct location. The RF terminal tells him which part or license plate (lot) to pick. If he scans an incorrect part or lot, the computer will know immediately.

He then goes to the next item and continues until the order is finished. The RF device will direct him to the appropriate staging or packing area (also bar coded), where he will leave the merchandise for packing. The computer will also track productivity, error rates, and idle time.

Each cart or pallet used for picking will also have a bar code label to track its location. Consider a cart or pallet a moving bin. The computer will know in what zones a picker is authorized to work. If he is not lift truck certified, you will not want to send him to pick an item that requires a lift truck.

Below are some sample screens for the picking process, with an explanation of how the picker will function. The picker will enter his identification code and choose a picking option.

```
PICKER_____

  PF1 - SCAN ITEM
  PF2 - BIN SEQUENCE
  PF3 - PART NUMBER SEQUENCE
  PF4 - ORDER SEQUENCE

ENTER RETURN TO END
```

PF1:   Scan Item: This option will be used if the picker is using a picking list (not the preferred method) instead of operating in a paperless environment.

PF2:   The picker will be directed through the warehouse in bin location sequence (preferred method).

PF3:   The picker will be directed through the warehouse in part sequence.

PF4:   The picker will be directed through the warehouse in order-line number sequence (i.e., how the order was entered).

If an order number is entered, it will be validated as an open order and then processed. If no order number is entered, the next order in the pick schedule will be processed. The pick schedule is a list of orders set up for picking based on requested date, customer priority, route or stop, or immediate pick in Order Entry.

For example, six orders were entered last week for tomorrow's delivery. A scheduling program examined the open order file and put these 6 orders into the to-be-picked file and flagged the orders that they were scheduled for picking. During the day, an inside salesperson enters an order at 10:00 am for today's delivery. It will be put in the schedule immediately (like an immediate print). If the pick date and request date are today, that order will go in front of the orders with a pick date of today and a ship date of tomorrow. The sequence of next order from the schedule is pick date, ship date, customer priority, route/stop.

To begin picking, the picker will choose a verification option:

```
ORDER NUMBER _____
BLANK = NEXT ORDER
PF1 - VERIFY BIN
PF2 - VERIFY PART
PF3 - NO VERIFICATION
PF4 - RETURN TO PICKER
       SCREEN
```

PF1 - to begin picking order with bin verification (verifies he is at correct bin).

PF2 - verification of the correct part number (to use this method all parts must be bar coded.)

PF3 - no verification (i.e., the bin or products are not bar coded).

PF4 - return to picker screen to end or change picking sequence.

The next screen to be displayed will be the order header information with pounds, cartons, and lines. Pressing enter will allow the picker to begin picking the order and display the first item to be picked. The picker can optionally preview the order before beginning, since he does not have any paper.

```
ORDER NUMBER  _____    XX/XX/XX
NAME
ADDRESS1        _____
ADDRESS2        _____
ADDRESS3        _____
SHIP VIA        _____


#XXXX X   CTN  XXXXX LN XXXXX
PF1 - PREVIEW ORDER    PF4 - VOID
```

On the next screen, the order number, line number, item, description, and bin will be displayed. If verification is turned on (either bin or part), the picker will scan the part or bin. If he has scanned a correct location or has scanned the correct item, the terminal will display the amount to pick in the correct unit of measure(s). The amount to pick can be overridden. If less is picked, a record will be created in the potential problem file for the inventory person to cycle count that item. Over-picking will require a security code to override.

```
ORDER NUMBER 123456        LN#    1
ITEM#         XXXXXXXXXX

DESCRIPTION   XXXXXXXXXXXXXXXX
XXXXXXXXXXXXXXXXXXXXXXXXXXXX

BIN    XXXXX
VERIFY         XXXXXXXXXXXX
PICK           3 CTN  5 EA
ENTER = NEXT PART, PF1 = STOP
```

If the picker only finds a portion of the items in this bin, the system will accept a lesser quantity and call up the item later with the unpicked quantity. This will allow the picker to continue in bin/part sequence and be directed to the overflow bin later. If the quantity per bin is being tracked, the system will tell the picker the quantity in the first bin.

When the picking is completed or if the picker presses PF1-Stop, the following screen will be displayed:

```
PF1 -    PRINT PACKING
         SLIP AND # LABELS _____
PF2 -    RETURN TO ORDER
PF3 -    STOP PICKING AND PRINT
         PACK SLIP - STAGE
         ORDER IN BIN XXXXX
PF4 -    CANCEL PICKING
```

If the picking is completed, the picker will press PF1 and a packing slip will print on the Shipping Department printer along with the number of labels, based on the quantity entered.

PF2 - Will allow the picker to return to the order in the event quit was entered accidentally. "ORDER NOT COMPLETE" will be displayed.

PF3 - Will stop picking and print a packing slip and/or labels for staging with bin location for tag and hold (assuming labels and bin were entered).

PF4 - Will cancel picking and undo anything done.

The order is now ready to be packed and/or staged for shipping.

Picking Summary

1. Do not print unnecessary documents. Paperless picking is a very important step and will require training and discipline.
2. The stock will be allocated to the order prior to picking, thus eliminating the chance of giving away stock promised to another customer without reallocating it.
3. The orders will be picked in the proper sequence based on due date and customer priority.
4. The picker's accuracy and productivity can be tracked.
5. If the items are bar coded properly and the order is entered properly, shipping the wrong item will be very difficult to do.
6. Credit memos and returns will be reduced dramatically.

PACKING/SHIPPING &
SHIPPING FEEDBACK/INVOICING

Packing/Shipping

The packer can scan the cart/pallet or a license plate of one of the items on the order. The computer knows:

1. how many pounds
2. how many boxes needed if repackaging
3. how many box labels
4. how it's being shipped
5. whether or not it is a hazardous material
6. if a bill of lading is needed
7. what's being shipped
8. value of shipment for insurance
9. if it is to be shipped COD

A packing slip will print with the correct items and quantities that are going to be shipped. Carton labels with the customer's ship-to address will also print. If the customer is EDI-capable, you can advise him what is being shipped via a shipping acknowledgment.

As a reengineered distributor, you will eliminate the need for multiple-ply packing slips. The only copy needed is the packing slip for the customer to go with the shipment. "What about my copy?" you ask. Why do you need a copy? You do not need it for invoicing. The quantity shipped has already been updated during picking. "What about my signed copy?" If it's shipped UPS, you do not get a signed copy back. If it's your truck, then the customer can sign a driver's manifest for the item he received. You can reproduce the packing slip on demand and also prove who signed for the delivery.

If the item is being shipped UPS or common carrier, each carton can be scanned and the shipping manifest system will automatically calculate the freight charges and write the tracker number for each carton back to the computer for traceability by customer PO number if the need arises.

Packing / Shipping Summary

1. No double checking of order for correctness.
2. All shipping documents will print automatically.
3. No delay in invoicing. Do not wait for a signed copy of the packing slip to invoice the shipment.
4. Do not print any internal copies of the invoice, regardless of how much the sales manager or accounting department screams. Use the computer.

Shipping Feedback/Invoicing

There is no need to manually invoice the order. The function is completely eliminated. The invoice (if required) is EDIed or faxed automatically to your customer if it did not go with the shipment. The computer has already been updated as to what was shipped during the picking and packing procedures.

A reengineered distributor does not need to print any copies of the invoice for internal use. With today's technology and the price of disk and CD-ROM, you will be able to keep seven years (or whatever is required by law) of history on your system. A customer invoice can be recalled instantly by anyone with a work station via order number, PO number, invoice number, or date, and viewed, reprinted, and/or faxed to the customer. Your savings will be approaching 63 cents per invoice. Internal copies serve absolutely no value.

Invoice Summary

1. You will eliminate the need to invoice an order after it is shipped. Let the system do it automatically.
2. The only copy of the invoice that needs to be printed is the one mailed to the customer, and only if he does not have a fax machine or is not capable of receiving invoices via EDI.

9

CENTRALIZED WAREHOUSING AND AUTO BRANCH REPLENISHMENT

Centralized warehousing is defined as a central or regional warehouse (or main location) that stocks other branches. The central warehouse is the primary path of replenishment for any particular branch, i.e., the branch does not normally buy from the vendor.

When should you use centralized warehousing? Some items can be purchased centrally and the branches replenished from a central warehouse or a main location, while the branch may buy other items directly from the vendor. There are advantages and disadvantages to both methods.

I remember a meeting I had with the CEO of a 250 branch distribution company. He asked me "How do you feel about branch managers purchasing their own materials?" I told him how I felt. "Branch managers do not necessarily make good purchasing agents. Their time should be spent servicing their customers and running their branch." He laughed and said, "I agree. Branch managers are (with inventory) like squirrels gathering nuts for the winter. Their input as to their unique market and what they should stock is important, but they should not do their own purchasing."

If you are using centralized inventory, there are a number of elements you must look at:

1. lead time of the item
2. cost of carrying inventory
3. cost of ordering
4. handling cost of merchandise for redistribution
5. distance between warehouses
6. centralized computer system for assistance

If those elements are favorable, there are definite benefits of centralized warehousing and purchasing:

1. eliminates excess stock in multiple branches
2. allows ability to carry less stock in branches
3. reduces duplicated safety stock
4. quantity discounts may be available, i.e., ability to order in carton quantities
5. freight allowances
6. cost of ordering may be reduced
7. leverage with vendor for larger orders, i.e., terms
8. ability to meet minimum order requirements
9. lower EOQ's

Before you jump into it, however, you should consider the following possible disadvantages of centralized warehousing:

1. lead time of redistribution
2. cost of redistribution
3. less stock in branches, chances of lost sales

I have found that centralized warehousing and pur-chasing have more advantages than disadvantages. Assuming they work for you, how do you do them? First and foremost, when you are calculating reorder points and EOQs for a central warehouse, you must look at all sales for the branches that are supplied by the central warehouse or main location.

In the example below, part A123 is stocked and sold out of eight locations. Location 01 buys directly from the vendor (3780). The lead time is 14 days and Location 01 sold 11. Note that Locations 02, 03, 04 and 08 each have a vendor number of 1. The vendor number of 1 means that they are sup-plied by Location 01 rather than directly from the vendor. Therefore, Location 01, who buys directly from the vendor, has a central usage of 36 - the eleven they sold plus ten from Loca-tion 02, five from Location 03, five from Location 04, and five from Location 08. Location 05 also buys directly from the vendor and supplies Locations 06 and 07. The central usage for Location 05 is 16. Location 05 sold six itself, and locations 06 and 07 each sold five.

Multi-Location Information

Part No.	Loc	Vendor	LT	AMU	Total Usage
A123	01	3780	14	11	36
A123	02	1		10	
A123	03	1		5	
A123	04	1		5	
A123	05	3780	14	6	16
A123	06	5		5	
A123	07	5		5	
A123	08	1		5	

Therefore in the next example, the ROP for Location 01 (the central supplier for Locations 02, 03, 04, and 08) is based on total sales (usage) of 36.

Assume:
* Item Class = A
* 50% Safety Stock
* 14 Day LT
* 7 day Vendor Review Time (VRT)

Location 1:

$$\left[AMU \times \frac{LT}{28} \times 1.50 \right] + \left[AMU \times \frac{VRT}{28} \right]$$

$$\left[36 \times \frac{14}{28} \times 1.5 \right] + \left[36 \times \frac{7}{28} \right]$$

$$27 + 9$$

$$ROP = 36$$

Location 05's ROP is based on total sales of 16

$$ROP = \left[16 \times \frac{14}{28} \times 1.5 \right] + \left[16 \times \frac{0}{28} \right]$$

$$\left[8 \times 1.5 \right] + \left[16 \times \frac{7}{28} \right]$$

$$ROP = 16$$

In the next example, the minimum stocking level (ROP) is 36 and the maximum (ROP + EOQ) is 49 for Location 01, and 16 and 25 for Location 05.

MIN-MAXs for Central Warehouses

Location	Vendor	AMU	ROP/ Minimum	Maximum
01	3780	11/36	36	49
02	01	10		
03	01	5		
04	01	5		
05	3780	6/16	16	25
06	05	5		
07	05	5		
08	01	5		

So how do we set stocking levels for branches? ROP and EOQ calculations do not work for branches that do not buy items directly from the vendor. There are no accurate lead times, and they can replenish as often as needed.

Centralized inventory assumes that the supplying warehouse will have the stock and can replenish its branches on a regular basis. You need to determine how often you are going to replenish them and then determine the number of months supply (or desired turn rate) you want them to have.

.50 month supply = 24 - 36 turns
.75 month supply = 18 - 24 turns
1.00 month supply = 12 - 18 turns
2.00 month supply =   6 - 9 turns

What I normally suggest is that you ask your branch manager, "We are going to send you a replenishment order twice a week (or as often as it is practical to send a truck). How many months' supply do you want as a maximum level?"

"Let's see," he will say. "You are going to replenish me twice a week?"

"Yes," you reply.

"Well," he will say, "a month's supply as a maximum will be plenty."

The next example shows the maximum based on one month, two months, or two weeks as a maximum branch factor multiplied by the AMU (Average Monthly Usage) of the branch.

BRANCH STOCKING LEVEL

AMU of Branch	x	Month Supply	=	Branch Max Level
5	x	1.0	=	5
5	x	2.0	=	10
5	x	.5	=	3

No EOQ is figured.

If you use a one month supply as a maximum, the minimum could be automatically calculated as one-half the maximum. If desired, a minimum branch factor could be used to calculate a minimum for the branch. The next example shows you the MIN/MAX for all locations based on the central usage as well as each branch.

Location	Vendor	AMU	ROP/ Minimum	Maximum
01	3780	11/36	36	49
02	1	10	5	10
03	1	5	3	5
04	1	5	3	5
05	3780	6/16	16	25
06	5	5	3	5
07	5	5	3	5
08	1	5	3	5

When all of the levels are set in the branches, you can use a push method of branch replenishment with automatic branch replenishment rather than the traditional costly pull method.

An automated branch transfer push system will create a transfer PO. The computer knows the available stock position in the branch and what they need on the next truck. It also knows the stock position of the main supplying location. The auto branch transfer will not deplete the central (supplying) warehouse's stock to supply the branch if the central warehouse is low (half of minimum or less).

If the central warehouse is low, the system should go into allocation mode:

1. If a branch has a demand, they will get whatever central has to satisfy the demand.
2. If the branch is below minimum (but no back order demand), they will get the percentage of the available stock that is proportional to their percent of the central's total average monthly usage (AMU).

EXAMPLE:

Available at Central = 10
Central's Total AMU = 22
Branch AMU = 5

Allocation of Available =   AVAIL x   Branch AMU
                                            Central's Total AMU

Allocation of Available =   10   x   (5/22)

2 will be transferred.

The system will not transfer the last unit from the central unless it is sold. Below is an example of how the available stock would be automatically allocated to each location in an automated push transfer system if the central supplying location was into safety stock.

LOC.	CENTRAL AVAIL.	X	(BRANCH AMU) (CENTRAL AMU)	=	TRANSFER AMOUNT	
1	10	X	5/22	=	(2.27)	2
2	8	X	9/22	=	(3.27)	3
3	5	X	2/22	=	(.45)	0
4	5	X	1/22	=	(.23)	0
5	5	X	5/22	=	(1.14)	1

Using an automated push transfer, the system will know the package quantity you have defined in the branch location record so that it will not suggest a transfer of three if there are five in a carton.

Imagine the smile on the branch manager's face when his fill rates are over 97.5% and the stock he needs shows up automatically, whether it be directly from the vendor or from the central warehouse.

In a reengineered distributor, the computer will create an automatic transfer for the branch on a regular replenishment cycle (weekly, bi-weekly, etc.) No one needs to walk the aisle, look at stock levels in the branch, or create a transfer. That's why the *process* is called auto-branch replenishment.

Centralized Warehousing and Auto Branch Replenishment Summary

1. The majority of purchasing and manual stock transfers required to be done by the branch are eliminated.
2. Branches are replenished more often, allowing higher turns and greater fill rates.
3. Excess stock is eliminated in the branch.
4. Branches can carry more items and will require less space.
5. The central warehouse can meet vendor minimums more frequently, which will result in lower ROPs due to the vendor review cycle discussed earlier.

10

THE SELLING PROCESS

Almost every distributor I have visited is sales dominated, i.e., "Do not mess with the sales manager," "This is the way we do things," or "NO, we can't change." Believe me, I have seen it all.

No matter what business you are in:

1. THE CUSTOMER IS KING.
2. HE MUST BE TREATED AS IF HE IS YOUR ONLY CUSTOMER.

However, a man must profess himself a poor merchant when he provides a quality product and the best service possible and gives away his profits to get the sale. And remember, a customer who does not pay his bills is not a customer.

Regardless of your business, there are some rules in reengineering the selling process that apply to most of you.

Rule #1

The role of the outside salesperson that takes orders and provides no value added services can usually be eliminated. The customer wants to reduce his cost of doing business, which means buying from you at a lower price. Salespersons who just take orders add little value and much cost, much like vendor salespersons discussed earlier. Eliminating the salesperson will allow lower prices without giving up profits.

Rule #2

Let the customer enter his own order whenever possible. He is doing the work and feels you are providing him a value-added service. Methods include Customer Remote Order Entry, EDI, PC Customer Order Entry with Imaging, and the Internet. The on-line Shopping Cart through the Internet is becoming as commonplace as the telephone. This not only eliminates salespersons and cost, it eliminates the majority of your Order Entry and Inside Sales Departments. (Note: we *did not* eliminate Customer Service.)

Rule #3

Never put telephones at your counter. If a customer comes to your place of business to be waited on personally and your counter person has to answer the phone to take an order or answer a question, the guy on the phone just "butted in line," and you encouraged it!

Rule #4

If you are going to welcome customers into your business to serve them, do not offend them with nasty signs. Imagine going to Wal-Mart, Home Depot, or Nordstrom's and seeing huge signs, "No Checks" or "If you bounce one it will cost you $25.00." How about this sign: "Welcome; buy from me, but if you make a mistake, I'm not taking it back unless you pay me a 15% restocking fee because I'm inefficient and/or you're stupid." Don't offend your good customers because of a few deadbeats.

I was on a flight from Chicago to Boston talking to a gentleman about his business. He said, "I am in the distribution business; sporting goods, to be specific." Of course, I was curious, so I asked him his sales volume. "Twenty-five million," he said willingly. "How many employees do you have?" was my next question. Of course, I was expecting the answer to be above 100. When he said about 25 I almost fell out of my seat. He has three hundred orders a day, 98% shipped via UPS, 900 customers, and an average order size of $350.

How in heaven's name could he do $25 million with 25 employees and ship any order that came in by 4:00 p.m. the same day? With further interrogation, I found out. He was not pulling my leg. He was a completely reengineered distributor, using technology to achieve his goals.

Three of his employees are programmers. He spent $1 million on technology. He has one order entry person. Ninety-six percent of his orders come in electronically, and are entered by his customers at their sporting goods stores on a PC he furnished if they did not already have one.

He has provided his customers with a tremendous service - a complete electronic catalog order entry system for their counter, complete with color pictures (images) of approximately 400 equipment items. (The 3,000 other items do not require pictures.) His customers can service their customers by entering the order, pricing it, and showing the product. The system also keeps track of the store owner's inventory. The store owner simply selects "send order" (stock and special orders) and the computer dials, sends the order, verifies delivery, sends back an acknowledgment, updates prices and AR balances, downloads any new items, etc. The invoice prints immediately. He has 99.5% inventory accuracy at the warehouse. The order is picked, packed, and shipped that day.

He also gets 10-12% higher margins and priority shipments from his three major suppliers because he prepays them for his estimated purchases of approximately $4 million a year each. This means no checks to cut. (If your revenue was $1 million per employee with the profits he has, you, too, could prepay your purchases.)

His competitors have more salespersons on the street, more inside salespersons and order takers, and less customer loyalty - you know, the traditional way.

One of my clients is an electrical distributor who gives his A and B customers a PC program, or a dumb terminal and modem if they do not have a PC. His customers can enter their own orders using a variety of look-ups as well as their own part numbers. He guarantees them the product will be on the job site by 8:00 am or available for will-call by 6:30 am for any order placed during the evening or the middle of the night. His favorite saying is, "I am making money while I am home sleeping." Until recently, he could only provide this service to the few who had PCs, and he needed a bank of modems for them to dial in. Today, he can allow all his customers complete access through their web browser over the Internet. It's as simple as ordering flowers.

Remember that 80-90% of your profits come from a select number of customers. Does everyone in your organization know who these customers are? In most organizations, it's probably only 10-20 customers. Every one of your employees needs to know them by name and be ready to jump through hoops to service them, especially if they need special attention or same day shipment.

Inside Sales/Customer Service

For those of you that do not have EDI, or electronically transmitted orders, you must have a great order processing system that will allow your people to service the customer instantly, in record time, with no need for call backs. A great order entry program can cut your person's time on the phone and at the counter by up to 75%. This in turn reduces your customer's cost of doing business with you, as well as your own costs.

Another client of mine is in the automotive aftermarket, selling heating and cooling products. His inside sales people have a one-day training program, and then they are "experts." The decision support system he uses makes them appear to be experts. He publishes his own catalog. Many of his customers call in, and are identified immediately by name, phone, zip code, or any portion of their name. If the customer has a catalog, he will order using the easy part number. Order processing is extremely fast, and if any accessories are needed, the computer alerts the order taker to inform the customer he should order a clamp with a hose, or a thermostat to go with the radiator.

If the customer does not have a catalog or does not know what part he needs, the decision support system leads the inside sales person directly to the part. The computer instructs the order taker to ask the year of the automobile, then displays all models available for that year. The computer knows the various engine sizes and transmissions, and tells the sales person the exact radiator needed, indicating availability, price, and companion items.

Based on the customer's zip code, the system also knows from which location the order will be filled: Chicago,

Atlanta, or Dallas. It knows if it will ship that day, based on total lines to be picked and picker availability.

Does your customer really want a *lower price*, or does he want *more profits*? How can you reduce his cost of doing business and still maintain your ROI (Return on Investment)? Look at reducing your complete channel costs, and pass on the savings.

Computer to Computer Communications

If your customer transmits his order directly from his computer to your computer, you will eliminate a tremendous amount of cost from the sales/order entry process. If your computer dials in daily, reviews his inventory, and extracts his order, you have eliminated his purchasing function. He has outsourced that expense to you.

Earlier we talked about VMI (Vendor Managed Inventory). Imagine the cost savings to your customer with DMI (Distributor Managed Inventory). Certain industries, Industrial and Hospital Supply, for example, are providing this service now. Why not pioneer it in your industry? "He won't let me do that!" you say. If your competitor provides that service before you do, it may be too late to save the account.

I have another client in the heating and cooling parts business who provides a service that allows his customers to eliminate the need for a warehouse to store parts and replenish their repairmen's trucks. My client keeps the inventory of each of his customer's trucks on his computer with MIN/MAX levels for each part on each truck. Their drivers go on calls, repairing furnaces or air conditioners. At the end of the day, they turn in their repair tickets for billing. The customer's computer transmits what was sold from each truck to my client's computer. A replenishment order is filled and put in a tote for each truck. The order can be picked up by the driver, or delivered to the customer's truck by the time the driver leaves in the morning. The customer no longer needs to keep inventory at the warehouse to replenish his own trucks. My client also provides his customers with a billing and accounting package that will handle their invoicing and accounts receivable as well as the seamless interface to their computer for the replenishment order.

Customer Options

Many distributors today offer their customers a menu of optional services, which will give the customer the ability to reduce his costs. For example:

MENU		
A. Salesman	No	Save 7%
B. Computer to Computer Order Entry	Yes	Save 3% (or cost to enter an order)
C. Automatic Ship - eliminate the cost of the customer's purchasing (Distributor Managed Inventory)	Yes	No charge
D. Electronic Funds Transfer	Yes	Save 3%
E. Financing	Yes	Add 1 1/2% / month
F. Direct Ship	Yes	Save 3%
G. Provide Customer with System (paid for through discounts)	Yes	Rebate

Those of you who are still thinking of equipping your salespersons with laptops so they can make a $250 sales call to take an order faster are, as Bruce Merrifield says, "paving over cow paths" instead of becoming part of the "Communications Super Highway." Bruce refers to this as "techno-waste."

Remember, you are *starting over.* You have no limitations, no manual systems, and unlimited technology. What menu of services will you offer your customer that will reduce his costs (and yours)?

Electronic Commerce and the World Wide Web

The Internet will become as important to your business in the next five years as the fax machine and the telephone. You can make your company, products, catalog, and ordering available to every potential customer in the world for next to nothing. By the year 2000, if not sooner, every one of your current customers and every potential customer will be searching for information and buying electronically. By the year 2002, 80% of our business transactions will be conducted using electronic commerce. ***Do not wait. This one tool will revolutionize the way you do business.***

Pricing

A very important part of the selling process is getting the right price for your products. Are you competitive on your commodity items? More importantly, are you getting the margin you need on the slower moving customer service items, or are you selling them too cheaply? A concept called Velocity Pricing is a way of improving your margins. Use velocity pricing to improve your margins on slow-moving items and customer service items. In addition, you will provide a very visible price advantage on the "A-est of the A's." (The A-est of the A's are commodity or highly-used items that everybody price shops. You need to be extremely competitive on these items.) The concept is that most customers price shop the fast movers (A items). Most distributors use matrix pricing by product group, which means they mark up a column a specific percentage from cost for an entire product line in order to be price competitive. For example, you might give a good customer pricing based on a 20% margin or markup on a specific product line. Within that product line there are A items on which you need to be competitive (that's why you only make 20%), but there are also C's, D's, and E's on which you're making 20%. Using velocity pricing can add "X" percent of gross profit to your bottom line because you are not giving away the slow movers in that product line.

In velocity pricing, there are two assumptions. First, customers price shop a limited amount of items in each line, and second, you provide the customer with his prices. You can't use velocity pricing if you try to discount off of a manufacturer's list price like everyone else. Bruce Merrifield wrote a very informative article titled, "List Price is Obsolete!" In this article, he discusses the origin of MLP (Manufacturer's List Price). "Many MLPs started during World War II and the late 40s when everything was on allocation and government price control affected all commodity materials." Bruce goes on to explain the negative side effects of high MLPs. Velocity pricing will not work if you use list prices and discount.

Once again, customers price shop two types of items: commodity items and high usage items. You need to be highly competitive in these two item groups. For example, if you are in plumbing, heating, and air conditioning, 1/2" copper fittings will be very visible "A" commodity items which customers will price shop. Customers compare most of your pricing to those few items on which they are aware of the competition's price. In a category like copper, without velocity pricing you might mark it up 22%. With velocity pricing, your computer system classifies your inventory for velocity pricing purposes into A, B, C, D, and E items. These categories represent the movement of items within a particular group. Velocity Pricing allows you to vary the margin you will receive on any particular item based on its classification. You may determine that a 21% margin on A items, which are high usage and very competitive, will give you a price advantage. However, you can mark up a B item 23%. On the C item, which is a customer convenience item and does not have the turns that you have on the A's and/or the Bs, you need to get a higher margin. The customer is just glad you have the D's, because you are a full line distributor. You may turn D items only twice a year. You could mark up D's 40% because on those items customers don't ask, "What's my price?"; they just call and say, "Do you have it? Great! Can you ship me one right away?" You need to generate higher margins on those items to support them on the shelf (turn and earn).

Example:

Category Class AA01

Without Velocity Pricing	With Velocity Pricing
22% Margin on all items	A - 21%
	B - 23%
	C - 30%
	D - 40%
	E - 47%

With velocity pricing, you can easily add 1 to 2% to your bottom line *and* your customer sees you as a price leader, i.e., you have the lowest price on the items he price shops. Yet you are getting a higher margin on the lower turn customer convenience items. Do not make the mistake of taking an entire product category and having a global markup for a particular price column, or you will give away a fair amount of your profits. When using velocity pricing, it helps to use flyers or to print your own price book that advertises a competitive price advantage for the high usage items. Of course, as a reengineered distributor, you will provide your customer with an electronic order system so he will not need a paper catalog.

Another pricing tool is called Combineability. Giving your customers an incentive to place larger orders can also reduce your costs. What this does is allow you to give customers quantity break pricing on similar items that can combine to meet a price break. Let's use wire as an example. You might have a quantity break on 5,000 feet of wire. However, a customer may not need to buy 5,000 feet of one item. You may give him a quantity break on any color wire within the same group. For instance, if he buys 500 ft. of red, 1,000 ft. of black, 2,000 ft. of yellow and 1,500 ft. of green, he will get the 5,000 quantity break price on all of the colors of wire he purchased.

Below is a sample of a price catalog offering quantity break pricing:

Quantity Breaks

All items in this group combine for Price Breaks	1 - 12	13 - 24	25 - Up
Item 1	12.96	11.75	10.95
Item 2	24.75	23.50	22.95
Item 3	32.47	31.07	29.95
Item 4	18.75	17.95	16.75
Item 5	7.85	7.25	6.98
Item 6	9.75	9.00	8.25
Item 7	15.27	14.96	14.50

One of my clients uses price combineability, but instead of quantity, the combineability is based on dollars of similar items of low value. To give his customers an incentive to place larger orders, he took things such as fittings, clamps, and other items that customers normally do not buy in large quantities and set up dollar volume price breaks. A customer who spends between $1.00 and $99 receives column one pricing, between $100 and $199, column two, etc. The price combineability on these items is on dollars and not on total units. This works effectively in certain lines. Below is a sample of a price catalog offering price combineability for dollar value:

Order Value Price Breaks

All items in this group combine for Price Breaks	$1 - $99	$100- $199	$200 - Up
Item 1	2.96	2.75	2.25
Item 2	4.75	4.50	3.95
Item 3	2.47	2.07	1.95
Item 4	8.75	7.95	6.75
Item 5	7.85	7.25	6.98
Item 6	9.75	9.00	8.25
Item 7	5.27	4.96	4.50

Commissions

Proper pricing is critical to the success and growth of your business. At the beginning of The Selling Process I said, "A man must profess himself a poor merchant when he provides a quality product and the best service possible and gives away his profits to get the sale." If you allow your salespeople to override prices within a specific gross margin range without prior approval, then they must be paid on gross profit, not on net sales.

The chart below shows examples of what you and your salesperson will receive if you pay him on gross profit versus on net sales.

Example	Price		Negotiated Price	
Sell	$1.35		$1.20	
Cost	1.00		1.00	
Profit	.35		.20	

10% Commission (paying on sales):

Salesperson Receives	$ .135	40%	$.12	60%
You Receive	.215	60%	.08	40%

If you sell your product for $1.35 and it costs you $1.00, you have a $.35 profit. Suppose you pay your salesperson on net sales on the $1.35. Your salesperson receives 13-1/2 cents and you receive 21-1/2 cents. However, if your salesperson lowers the price to $1.20 and your cost is still $1.00, the profit is 20 cents. If you paid him on net sales, he would get commission on the $1.20 instead of the $1.35, which means he would receive 12 cents, reducing your share of the 20 cents profit to 8 cents. In this example, he receives 60% of the revenue and you only receive 40% to cover your expenses and overhead. As you can see, if he sold it for $1.35, you would get the majority of the profit; however, once he reduces the price, the tables turn dramatically.

38% of GP (paying on GP):

Salesperson Receives	$ .135	40%	$.074	40%
You Receive	.215	60%	.126	60%

115

In the above example, you're paying him on gross profit, and he receives 38% of the gross profit. If he sold it for a 35 cent profit, he would receive 13-1/2 cents and you would receive 21-1/2 cents (the same as the example where he is paid on net sales at 10%). However, under the gross profit scenario, when the price is reduced to $1.20, your salesperson receives 7.4 cents and you receive 12.6 cents, so you still get 60% of the margin. If you let your salespeople negotiate price, it is imperative that you pay them on gross profit and not net sales.

Another method to ensure that you're getting the highest margin available is to implement a system called Sliding Scale Commission. This allows you to vary the percent of commission if your salesperson discounts the product.

Sliding Scale Example

Gross Profit %	% of Earned Commission
100%	150%
70%	135%
60%	125%
40%	120%
35%	100%
25%	90%
20%	80%
19%	60%
10%	00%

In the sliding scale example, if he sells your product for between 25% and 35% profit, he receives 100% of his earned commission on the profit (whatever percentage that may be). But if he lowers the selling price so that your margin is 25% or 20%, he receives 90% or 80% of his commission, and so forth.

In this example, he is not only getting paid on gross profit, he is getting paid on declining percent as the gross profit declines. On the other hand, if he sells it for over 35% you may elect to give him 100+% of his commission, i.e., giving him an incentive to sell it at a higher price whenever possible.

Counter Sales

I have another client who has reengineered the traditional warehouse concept. Many of you have a fair amount of will-call or counter sales. You have a large warehouse and a counter with a relatively small store area for your customers to pick up those impulse items.

This client decided to open up the majority of his warehouse and make it a supermarket. It's like a Home Depot just for contractors. The contractor can either go shopping on his own and return to the checkout just like Home Depot, or he can be accompanied by a counter person who has an RF (Radio Frequency bar code reader) unit. He scans the items as the contractor selects them. When he is finished shopping, his order is already entered and ready to print when he gets to the counter. What a novel idea; put the warehouse in front of the counter and don't make your customer stand in line to check out. This client has grown 40% a year in an industry that is relatively flat.

Earlier we discussed how you did not need to file a copy of the signed packing slip if the product is delivered. What about the on-account customer who comes in to pick up some items? Simple. You have him sign for his order on an electronic signature capture pad. The one-ply ticket will print with his signature and it will be captured on unalterable media so it can be reproduced if anyone refuses to pay the bill because they do not have a copy. Electronically fax it to them, signature and all. Also, a list of people authorized to charge will be brought up for that customer. Their signature can be verified electronically. It *cannot* be forged.

Selling Summary

1. Remember the rules of what makes a customer, and once you determine he is a valued customer, treat him like one. *Everyone* in your organization must treat him that way.
2. Do not add unnecessary costs to the channel by using salespersons if they are not needed, by overpaying them, or by using a complex pricing structure.
3. Give your customers information electronically, and make it easy for them to do business with you.
4. Remember that you are not just selling products, you are providing services. How can you reduce your customer's cost of doing business, not just sell him at a lower price?
5. Set up your web page and allow your customers to shop and place orders as simply as possible.

11

EDI

EDI (Electronic Data Interchange) is defined simply as computer to computer communication. EDI deals with ANSI standards known as X.12. This format allows the sending and receiving of documents to your trading partners (vendors and customers) through a mail box service known as a VAN (Value Added Network). EDI can also be done directly to your trading partner or through the Internet.

In the near future, the distributor, the customer, and the vendor will need to be EDI compliant in order to remain competitive. This will result in tremendous savings through reduced labor costs, additional information in a timely manner, and increased accuracy. Can you imagine the savings if:

1. all of your customers transmit their orders via EDI
2. you EDI a confirmation verifying delivery date, availability, and price
3. you EDI a shipping confirmation and invoice, and
4. they EDI you a remittance advice and wire transfer the money?

The same process can take place between you and your vendors.

What if your customer EDIed you what he sold so you could replenish him automatically, and you then EDIed your vendor your daily sales so he could produce, replenish, and forecast more accurately. Many companies have avoided EDI like the plague, and have seen much cost with little return. EDI will not be justified for only one customer or vendor. If the majority of your vendors and/or customers participated, however, the savings could indeed be tremendous.

The most common EDI document that distributors use is an 850 in and an 850 out. An 850 from your customer to you is a purchase order out for him and a sales order in for you. Likewise, if you create a purchase order to your vendor and EDI it to him, then an 850 is a purchase order out for you and a sales order in for him. Trying to retrofit EDI into your old computer system can be costly. Make sure that the technology you use is fully EDI compliant and seamlessly integrated with the system. In the past, some companies were up against the wall because their biggest customer(s) said, "If you are not ready to receive our orders via EDI by January 1, you will not get our business." They ran out and bought an EDI system on a PC and received the customer orders into their building via EDI. However, there was no connection to their in-house system. They printed the orders and re-keyed them into the system. (We refer to this as RIP and READ.) THIS IS NOT EDI. They left themselves open to a chance for a data entry error. It would have been cheaper for the customer to fax the order!

EDI is computer to computer communication. Below are two flow charts depicting the steps involved in both processes. You can clearly see the difference.

TRADITIONAL PAPER METHOD

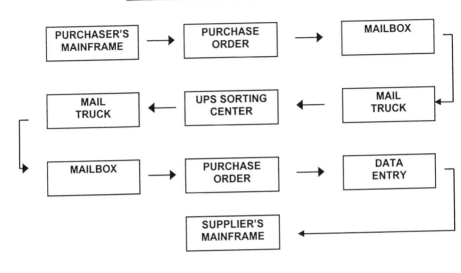

WITH EDI

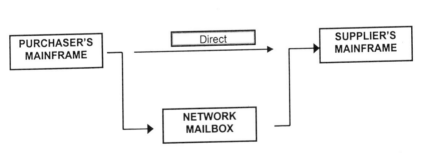

EDI will eliminate the possibility of any input errors and eliminate the need for any input costs. The savings can be phenomenal.

Wal-Mart, Lowes, and other major chains have lowered their cost of doing business using all the EDI transaction sets available to accomplish VMI (Vendor Managed Inventory). These companies have coined the term QR (Quick Response). With today's technology and more of your vendors investing in EDI, you, too, can implement VMI or QR. (Why should the big guys have all the fun?!)

12

EXPEDITING

Auto Expediting can allow you to detect a potential delivery problem before it happens. An expediting process should review all customer open orders and back orders and analyze available stock as well as open purchase orders to see if a problem does or will exist with a delivery date.

Suppose a customer orders ten widgets with a request date of 10/12/9X. The system knows that:

A. you have the stock and everything is okay
    or
B. you do not have it but you have it on order
    or
C. it is a special order.

Let's suppose you do not have the stock, so you order it. The customer requirement is covered for quantity, but does anyone check to see if the vendor delivery date is compatible with the customer requested date? An automated expediting system will check to see if the stock coming in will arrive in time to be delivered to the customer by the requested date.

Using digital faxing and electronic mail, an expediting system will find any problems that are going to occur and fax the vendor a memo stating "PO number 'X,' Item 'X' needs to be shipped on 'X' date to satisfy our customer's ship date. Its current ship date will cause it to be 'X' days late. Please contact our buyer to discuss if anything can be done." Internally, the buyer is notified of the potential problem via E-mail, and the customer service person assigned to the customer is also E-mailed. This process closes a potential loophole, and is a prime example of a reengineered process using technology to cross departmental boundaries.

13

DATABASE MARKETING

Many of you are sitting on a gold mine but do not realize it. That gold mine is information. Retailers have been using database marketing for years to target the right products to the right customers. For years you have thrown away virtually every piece of information about your products and customers. Look at your top customers - those who generate the highest profits. What are the common links - size, number of employees, type of business, location, salespersons, etc.? Database marketing allows you to keep a comprehensive database on every customer. If you knew what your customer needed and when, you could cater to him. In addition, you need to know everything there is about the company, the owners, and the buyers and users of your products and services.

Currently, most distributors use product information in a singular dimension, i.e., strictly for replenishment and reorder points. Your product information, however, is available in a four-dimensional format. The four dimensions are product, combined with customer, combined with price, and time. What, who, how much, and when. Based on a customer's primary business, what products should he be buying? If a large contractor buys "X" amount of widgets at this price weekly, then shouldn't all customers that meet that profile be buying similar items, in about the same quantity, at about the same price, at about the same time? With this data, you could service your current customers more effectively, profile the perfect customer, and use that data to target new customers.

With an integrated marketing module, any of your people who have communications with customers could have a wealth of information available at their fingertips.

A fully-integrated customer marketing module can provide much more than just product information. You can track characteristics on every company and every contact within that company. You can mail a letter or call every customer or prospect that has any identifying trait or characteristic coupled with any other element(s) of data. For example, you can tell the computer to schedule an activity (call, visit, mail) for a person (you or someone else) for any customer or prospect who has less than 30 employees, buys more than 'X' dollars of blue widgets in the state of Illinois, and plays golf.

You are beginning to see that he who holds the information wins. You should have access to information that will provide instant answers to questions such as:

- Is this customer an asset to your organization or a liability?
- Considering his primary business, what product categories should he be buying versus what product categories he is buying?
- When does he place orders and how often?
- Should your salesperson be calling him on a particular day at a particular time?
- What are his hot buttons, how does he pay, what is the service level you are providing him?
- Does he have any open quotations?

Identify the top 10-20 customers that make up the majority of your profits, and make sure everyone in your organization knows who they are. Likewise, try to rid yourself of the bottom 20% that add much cost and little margin. There are many hidden costs. Things such as returns, last minute small orders, price shopping, cancellation, low order-to-estimate ratios, slow payment, and a demanding customer that causes havoc within your entire organization are hassles you can do without. A customer's lack of profitability may be disguised by volume.

Before you can provide superior service to your good customers, you must know who they are, and then use your database marketing to find new ones just like them.

With the price of disk and the availability of database tools, data warehousing is something in which every distributor should invest.

THE CREDIT FUNCTION - CUSTOMER RANKING

Have you ever had to borrow money from a bank? Why do they always want to see a current aging of your AR? The same reason you do. You know if the invoice is over 90 days old, it's in jeopardy. Over half of the companies in the Fortune 500 at the beginning of 1980 are no longer in business today. If it can happen to the big guys, it can happen to your customers. Remember this: "A customer who does not pay his bill is not a customer." Make sure your salespersons (if you insist on keeping them) know this. In fact, the reengineered distributor pays commission on paid invoices, not on sales or shipments.

I believe that the majority of the credit function, which is now a costly, time-consuming function, can be highly automated. Have you ever exceeded your credit limit on your credit card, or made an unusually large purchase? I have! It did not take a human being to reject my sale. The computer did it automatically. Most distributors have one or more very important people called Credit Managers who determine whether or not an order will be released for shipment. If that person is gone for the afternoon, everything comes to a halt. Just like ROP and EOQs, credit limits, allowable past due amounts and days, and order limits can be set automatically based on the data the computer has on the customer, his payment history, and average order size. The computer knows:

1. payment history
2. average days to pay
3. average order size
4. credit rating
5. volume of business
6. date of last payment
7. amount of last payment

I have a client who receives 12,000 credit approval holds per month. Their credit department releases all but 400 of them. With some artificial intelligence, they cut those credit approval holds to a fraction of what they were.

The computer can generate credit limits and check past due balances. The average monthly sales and your allowable days to pay, times a credit rating multiplier, can automatically generate the credit limit.

The formula for calculating the credit limit is:

$$CL = AMS \times \frac{ADP}{30} \times (1 + CRM\%)$$

where
- CL = Credit Limit
- AMS = Average Monthly Sales
- ADP = Acceptable Days to Pay
- CRM = Credit rating multiplier %

Based on the customer rating, you can have a table to determine the acceptable days to pay and the credit rating multiplier % for A, B, C, D, and E customers.

Customer Rank	CRM %	ADP
A	100	45
B	75	45
C	50	30
D	25	30
E	0	10

If the customer rating is A (excellent), then you may want a credit rating multiplier of 100%. If it is C (good), you may want a credit rating multiplier of 50%.

Example: AMS = $10,000   (average monthly sales)
            ADP =   45   (acceptable days to pay)
            CRM =   100%   (credit rating multiplier)

$$CL = 10,000 \times \frac{45}{30} \times (1 + 1.00)$$

$$CL = 15,000 \times 2$$

$$CL = \$30,000$$

Using this formula, the credit limit will be $30,000.

If the ADP (acceptable days to pay) is 30 and the credit rating multiplier is 50%, then the credit limit will be $15,000.

$$CL = 10,000 \times \frac{30}{30} \times (1 + .50)$$

$$CL = 10,000 \times 1 \times 1.5$$

$$CL = \$15,000$$

The computer can then credit hold any order automatically based on the credit limit. The computer can also do a past due check in addition to the credit limit check. The past-due check can vary by customer. For example, if the customer is a municipality and always pays, but it takes them forever to do so, you may want to turn off the past-due check for that customer. But what about the rest of them? You may want to let an excellent customer's order be processed even if he has a 90 days past-due balance.

Most systems will check to determine if the customer is 60 days past due, and if so will place the order on credit hold. Then the credit manager becomes involved and makes an emotional decision. Based on the ADP (acceptable days to pay) and the average days to pay, plus the customer rating, you can have the computer do the work for you. For example, if an excellent customer has a credit limit of $30,000 and usually pays within 45 days with average monthly sales of $10,000, his aging should look like this:

Current	Over 30	Over 60	Over 90	Over 120
10,000	5,000	0	0	0

If he had an aging of:

Current	Over 30	Over 60	Over 90	Over 120
10,000	10,000	8,000	0	0

would you credit hold the order? Maybe, maybe not. Set the rules and take the guesswork out of the majority of the credit decisions.

In the example below, the computer would hold the order if the customer had a past-due balance of $10,000 over 90 days, but release the order if the past-due amount was only $200 over 90 days.

Hold	Current	Over 30	Over 60	Over 90	Over 120
Y	10,000	5,000	8,000	10,000	0
N	10,000	5,000	4,000	200	0

The past-due hold of over 30, 60, 90 and 120 should be a percentage of the AMS (average monthly sales) based on the customer rating.

Customer Rating	Over 30	Over 60	Over 90	Over 120
A	150%	50%	10%	0%
B	125%	50%	5%	10%
C	100%	25%	0%	0%
D	100%	10%	0%	0%
E	50%	10%	0%	0%

For example, this method will allow an order to go through if that 'A' customer with average monthly sales of $10,000 has a past-due balance of less than $1,000 past 90 days and less than $5,000 past 60 days. The computer should also check the size of the order in relation to his average order size. If the customer credit limit is $15,000 and his average order is $500, you may want to look at a $5,000 order. Using this method for credit limit, order size, and past due will allow you to automate your credit function. The credit manager will then deal only with the true problems. The order entry person should be able to enter the order (or if the order comes in electronically the order is accepted), but if it fails the three credit checks discussed, then the order will appear on the credit manager's screen for a decision.

Credit Card Authorization

Many distributors are accepting credit cards as a viable type of payment. They are preferred over COD in many instances. If you accept credit cards as a preferred type of payment, then your computer can store the customer's card number(s), auto dial to get the authorization code, and automatically accept the card without any extra work.

15

PEOPLE POWER

While technology is a necessary element of reengineering, the most essential component of your plan is your people. The only sustainable advantage any company has is its people. You cannot reengineer without good people and good leadership. You must function as the coach, and you need the best players possible. You need to have a strong vision of what you want to do, and you need to be certain that your vision is clear to everyone. The goals of the company must be definable, measurable, and manageable.

Goals and results (including the numbers) must be posted for everyone to see. People take pride in what they do. The entire company must be:

A. <u>CUSTOMER DRIVEN</u> - This is extremely important. Everyone must agree that the customer is KING. As mentioned earlier, your people must be willing to do whatever it takes to make your customers happy. Without customers, you don't need anything else we have discussed in this book!

B. <u>EMPOWERED</u> - Allow your people to make decisions when faced with what has been called "the moment of truth." Making a customer wait through multiple decision levels, or until someone "with authority" is available is not in keeping with "The Customer is King" policy.

C. <u>PROCESS FOCUSED</u> - The people with some of the best suggestions for streamlining processes are the people who actually perform the tasks. Encourage your people to focus on what they do, and encourage them to make (and/or reward them for making) suggestions to improve processes.

D. <u>QUALITY CONSCIOUS</u> - Quality is mandatory in any business. Your products, your service, and your people and their attitudes must all be of superior quality if you are going to attract and retain the kinds of customers who will allow you to be profitable.

Imagine that you were starting a brand new company and interviewing everyone on your staff for a position with that company. How many would you re-hire? You need to surround yourself with quality people who believe in your product, your company, and your goals. Anyone who is not part of your team needs to be replaced.

The only things that differentiate you from your competitors are your people, your vision, your values, and your ability to adapt to change.

16

IN CONCLUSION

Reengineering is not for everyone, but hopefully this book shed some light on the potential gains from improving (simplifying) your processes. I suggest you and your staff read it a number of times. Each time, take one idea or one process and determine how your company can implement that idea or process. I firmly believe that technology is the primary vehicle that will allow you to get where you want to go.

Reengineering will take time and require a capital investment in technology. Before you make any capital investment, make sure you have the answers to the following questions:

1. Will it increase sales?
2. Will it reduce costs or increase employee productivity?
3. Will it get me a better return on assets (turn and earn)?
4. Will it improve customer service?

If the answer to any of these is yes, then do it.

Gene Roman has been involved in the design and implementation of software systems for over 20 years, specializing in Inventory Management, Warehousing, and On-line Customer Service. As CEO and founder of Systems Design, Inc., a twenty-three-year-old company that provides technology solutions to the distribution industry, he has provided consulting services and practical advice to hundreds of distributors. He possesses a definite hands-on knowledge of every aspect of the distribution industry.

Mr. Roman, who earned an MBA in business management from DePaul University, Chicago, is the author of *The Key to Profit* and *Increasing Your Bottom Line*, as well as numerous articles on inventory, computer selection, and increasing profits which have appeared in trade journals and industry publications. He presents seminars and workshops nationwide dealing with Inventory Management, Technology and the Automated Warehouse, Customer Service, Competing with Technology, Electronic Commerce, and Reengineering the Distributor, and has been a guest speaker for numerous trade associations.